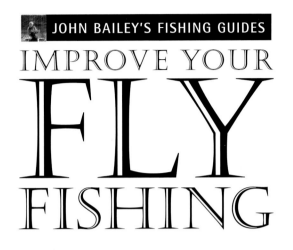

JOHN BAILEY'S FISHING GUIDES

IMPROVE YOUR
FLY
FISHING

JOHN BAILEY'S FISHING GUIDES

IMPROVE YOUR
FLY
FISHING

LEARN THE UNDERWATER SECRETS OF FISH AND THEIR HABITATS

First published in 2003 by
New Holland Publishers (UK) Ltd

London • Cape Town • Sydney • Auckland

www.newhollandpublishers.com

10 9 8 7 6 5 4 3 2 1

Garfield House, 86–88 Edgware Road, London W2 2EA

80 McKenzie Street, Cape Town 8001, South Africa

14 Aquatic Drive, Frenchs Forest, NSW 2086, Australia

218 Lake Road, Northcote, Auckland, New Zealand

ISBN 1 84330 346 9

Edited and designed by Design Revolution Limited,
Queen's Park Villa, 30 West Drive, Brighton BN2 2GE
Project Editor: Ian Whitelaw
Designer: Lindsey Johns
Editor: Julie Whitaker
Illustrations by Rob Olsen

Index by Indexing Specialists,
202 Church Road, Hove BN3 2DJ

Publishing Manager: Jo Hemmings
Senior Editor: Kate Michell
Assistant Editor: Anne Konopelski
Production Controller: Lucy Hulme

Reproduction by Pica Digital (Pte) Ltd, Singapore
Printed and bound in Singapore by Craft Print
(Pte) Ltd

Contents

INTRODUCTION

I first watched trout feeding in the crystal-clear river at Dovedale in the English Midlands; my diary tells me the year was 1958 and, at my behest, journeys to the river that summer became something of a Sunday family ritual. By 1960, I was fly fishing myself, this time at Tintwhistle reservoir in Derbyshire's Peak District. For a long while I was spectacularly unsuccessful; my tackle was borrowed or begged, and I only realized later that it was fatally ill-matched. A slight greenheart fly rod was allied with a savagely sinking salmon line and, as I'd only heard of dry-fly fishing, the combination was without hope. I can't even begin to think of the number of tins of grease I used up trying to make that line float.

▲ **ALL STIRRED UP** Murky water is a constant problem, especially in the northern hemisphere. Fish can stir the bottom silt whilst wind, rain and algal blooms can all ruin a well-laid plan.

▲ **PICTURED FROM BELOW** Here you see Kevin Cullimore photographing me as I land a Sussex trout. My association with Kevin was a vital step in the germination of this book.

Tintwhistle reservoir in those days was perfectly clear with high surrounding banks. During the weekdays of the school holidays, fishing pressure was minimal and I began to recognize more and more that the trout chose to come into the bank to feed whenever they could. I'm not really certain of the reason – perhaps it was because Tintwhistle was a poor water and they were feeding on terrestrials. Whatever the cause, I realized that all I needed to do was to get a floating fly a couple of feet from the bank and not disturb the trout.

That's how it was for two years: I'd choose a good vantage point, mark down a few feeding fish and then skilfully and silently creep my way into position. If I could ease out a dry fly even six or twelve inches from the bank without having to put any of the dreaded line on the water, then I was in with a good chance. In fact,

in those heady days I rarely failed to take home a proud little bag limit. For years I hardly caught a trout more than two feet from the bank. I don't know how ethical this all is, but I do know it quickly taught me the paramount importance of watching fish, their water and their food, and how the three elements function as a whole.

EVERY PICTURE TELLS A STORY

From 1970 onwards, I kept trout in tanks for close-up study, and I have spent much of my life on the river-bank observing trout in the water. In 1998, however, I added yet another dimension to my observations of fish behaviour and the underwater habitat. I learned to dive, and have now spent many hours under water with a camera. What follow are 160 or so images that have been taken either under the water or very close to the action from above, or are of my fish tank. I like to think that most of the shots are important and that all tell a message. What I can't do is pretend that a camera can ever tell you everything, and there are a good many lessons that no film can capture.

SOUND ADVICE

Having lain in the water and watched trout respond to external stimuli, I can tell you that the sounds you make can certainly prove fatal to your chances of a catch. Be extremely mindful of that heavy boot step on gravel or stone. Refine the fall of your fly line until it settles with a whisper. Do not talk loudly with your friends. I've watched pools empty due to idle chatter. Electric motors, careful rowing, slow and gentle movements... try to be as quiet a presence on the bank as you possibly can. The heron hasn't developed his behavioural strategies for nothing.

You don't have to spend very long diving to realize that water is three-dimensional. A river is not a mechanical escalator taking water to the sea. Rather, it has innumerable quirks and characteristics, always on the move, with ever-dancing currents. Still waters, too, have their own pushes and pulls beneath the surface, even though they are often more subtle.

It is how a fly is fished relative to the water that is all important. A fly may look quite fantastic in the still water by your feet, but how is it going to work when the currents are pushing and pulling it. If it's going to have any impact at all, you need to put that fly in its fishing context.

▼ KEEPING IT SIMPLE Full scuba gear is not always necessary to study fish in their natural habitat. If the weather is warm and bright, T-shirts, shorts and goggles will suffice.

So, watch the water carefully and thoughtfully to build up some picture of its complexities. As a rule, fish with as short a line as possible. If you need to fish long, it may be because you've pushed the fish there in the first place.

Although I'm not a fish scientist, I am quietly convinced from what I've seen that salmon and trout respond to colours, at least to some degree, and that they can see things sharply to a very considerable extent. One or two fly writers in the past, notably Peter O'Reilly, have used the word 'tone' to describe the colours these fish might see, and there's no doubt that some colours do merge into the background better than others and are, therefore, much less obtrusive. Black and shades of grey certainly blend in well in Irish waters, so it's no real wonder that half the Irish guides I've talked with recently would kick off with a black fly ninety per cent of the time. However, as you'd probably guess, above all it's movement that appears to be the trigger. Move any fly well and you're in with a chance.

I would also advise that you really do keep up to speed with the whirlwind developments that are occurring in the fly-fisher's tackle market. New lines and leaders are especially worth keeping an eye on. Anything that presents a fly more gently and less obviously is to be encouraged, so do try out new products. From what I've seen beneath the surface, our presentation of flies is far from perfect but, thanks to technological advances, it's certainly better than it would have been a quarter of a century ago. Braid, fluorocarbon, copolymer... be sure to try them all, because they can make a great difference to your fishing.

ACTING FOR THE BEST

Back when I was a child, every fish was inevitably killed, and I've lost count of the number of bags full of dead, discoloured corpses that I've either seen or hauled home myself. I really do believe, however, that the world is changing, and that more and more anglers are

taking on board the impact that they can have on any watercourse. As anglers, we don't do nearly as much damage as the nets at sea do, but the sea trout or salmon that we have just caught has actually made it back to its natal stream and is in a position to spawn. This is the survivor, and shouldn't it be allowed to play its role? I can clearly remember my Irish guide on Lough Corrib lamenting the number of fish taken during the mayfly season – he said simply, 'We've got wild fish in Ireland at the moment, a good number of them. We don't want to make your English mistakes and lose the lot.' Well, England hasn't actually lost the lot, but it very nearly did. Let's recognize the fact that when we fish we can have an impact for good or for ill.

FOR THE TECHNICALLY-MINDED ANGLER

I won't go into the intricacies of diving equipment here: a standard dry suit and the usual diving equipment is all that is needed. Extra-heavy weights are sometimes vital to keep you on the bottom. Less important are flippers – most of the time is spent simply sitting and waiting on the bottom of the river-bed!

▲ **TRIGGER POINT** These small warm-water fish are almost invisible to predators… apart from that giveaway black eye – their one undoing. When choosing a fly, bear this in mind and look for patterns that emit a subtle signal, a target.

I have used Nikon F90Xs exclusively with a range of Nikon lenses. The most useful have been 24mm and 28mm. I have generally used the Nikon speed light SB-28 when extra light has been needed. For a lot of the work I have used a Subal metal unit; this is very solid and trustworthy. For lighter, more mobile work I use a Ewa-marine plastic bag; this may sound a bit flimsy, but it has only let me down once! Films have been uniformly Fuji; Provia 100 has been preferred, but at times of low light I've moved to 200 ASA or 400 ASA speeds.

I hope that some of my underwater observations will throw light on the challenges that we, as anglers, meet on fly-fishing waters everywhere. Good luck.

John Bailey, Salthouse, Norfolk

CRYSTAL CLEAR

The crystal-clear waters of the world offer the greatest challenges, problems and excitements. Gin water brings the very best out of any angler for a glaringly obvious reason: the trout, grayling, char or salmon can see everything with pin-point accuracy. In England, the clearest waters are probably to be found in the Wessex chalk streams. Lord Grey describes fishing this area in his epic book *Fly Fishing*: 'These Winchester trout taught us the necessity of using fine gut and small flies and of floating the fly accurately over a rising fish: but they did more than that; they taught us to expect success only as a result of patience and hard work.'

The anglers who fish pellucid streams in South Africa, New Zealand, America and parts of Europe know this only too well. There are, however, always ways round any fishing problem. Take your time, watch the water and look for the right strategy.

▲ **PLANNING THE DAY** Simon and Mick sit down and ponder this Greenland valley. Don't rush into any fishing situation, even on a virgin water. Take time to analyze the water and the best potential approaches.

Greenland

Water just doesn't get clearer than it is in Greenland. Most of the rivers run straight from the ice-cap itself, so the water is frighteningly pure along virtually all the river systems. These rivers are host to vast runs of sea-going Arctic char, which are returning to their native rivers to spawn. The fishing is fabulous, and each tide introduces fresh pulses of fish to enthral the angler. As they move upstream, it's almost as though a thick silver carpet is lying across the river. New fish also mean fish that have not seen a fly before.

The place to appreciate the scale of the migration will be at the tail of a pool just up from long rapids. Any migratory species will choose to rest here, and char are no exception. In water that's often only eighteen inches deep, you can see the fish as they reassemble and take a metaphorical deep breath before moving on towards the spawning redds. Although straight in from the sea, some of the males will already be developing those crimson stomachs that make the char so exotic.

▲ PARADISE Waters as clear as this are hugely stimulating for an angler as they allow him or her to watch every movement of the fly and the fish's reaction to it. There are rules to be observed, however: enter the water carefully; check the angle and position of the sun, and consider your shadow; cast as discreetly as possible; always wear Polaroids and a peaked cap to help reduce outside light from penetrating.

◀ **A Travelling Shoal** Working under water in Greenland is not easy as the water temperatures are rarely much above freezing. Here, we can see a travelling shoal of char. We know they're travelling because they are widely spaced, milling around the pool, constantly in search of an exit. These are fish that will take a lure-type fly worked very quickly through them. They're very active, very aggressive and very territorial.

◀ **A Tight Shoal** By contrast, these fish are densely packed, forming a virtual cloud of fish in the water, all moving together. This shoal is located well upriver, near the ice-cap where the fish are ready for spawning. A lure in situations like this hardly seems to work at all as the char refuse to follow. Instead, a nymph worked through them produces an instant take.

◀ **Slowly Does It** The nymph must be worked at exactly the depth of the fish, because they are unwilling to either rise or fall in the water for food that they're not particularly interested in. You really need to work it past their very noses – this means accurate casting and a clear sense of what the underwater currents are doing. Also expect the most delicate of takes; for this reason a strike indicator may be useful.

▲ **PERFECTION** All fish are designer-made, hand-crafted for their environment, but the char is something special. The body shape is perfectly streamlined for the quick waters and strong sea currents that they have to negotiate. Note the size of that dorsal fin, a vast propeller to send them up waterfalls gushing from the eternal ice. You can see marks of what is probably net damage on this fish. The local Inuit people trap fish in the fjord as they enter the river, they then smoke the fish to see them through the winter; it's a traditional practice and the Inuit only take a small percentage of the harvest.

▶ **QUICK RELEASE** It's imperative with all fish, if you're going to return them, to get them back into the water as quickly as possible. The blood is already beginning to drain from the snout of this char even though it's only been out of the water for a matter of seconds. As you return the fish, hold it steady in the current and don't grasp that fin root too firmly or its delicate bone structure will be dislodged. The fish will make its own mind up when it's strong enough to breast the current.

New Zealand

New Zealanders, Americans, South Africans and Australians have developed some excellent skills over the years to cope with the most challenging fish in difficult, clear-water environments. Very frequently, these anglers have learned their skills in isolation from the perceived wisdom of the 'Old World' and, as a result, they have pioneered some highly effective flies, techniques and approaches. In New Zealand I was in awe, not so much of fly design, but of just how deftly and athletically my guides approached the thin, clear rivers that we were fishing. Often, this did not involve fly fishing in the accepted, English chalk stream tradition. The anglers wriggled, squirmed and climbed trees; they used every available shred of cover and, if there wasn't any, they moved with the patience of a heron. This was an all-out, guerrilla-warfare type of fishing, which I personally adored. It's very physical, and hard work in the heat, but it certainly catches fish.

▲ EMERALD LAKES From my observations below the surface, fish lead very ordered lives and do not like to break their routines unless they are forced to for any one of a number of reasons. The great advantage of very clear lakes such as these is that you can watch individual fish and establish their patrol routes. You can even ambush them: lay a fly on the bottom, wait for the fish to approach and then twitch it at the appropriate moment. Perhaps not for the purist, but thrilling all the same and a method that demands a great deal of fish knowledge.

▶ MIGRATION I would advise anyone new to New Zealand to hire a qualified guide for at least part of their stay. The reason is simple: the vast waterways of New Zealand hold numbers of trout like these whose behavioural patterns are very difficult for the newcomer to decipher. They migrate up and down rivers in ways that are quite baffling unless you're a local. You may know one water very well indeed, but that does not mean to say that all environments behave in exactly the same manner.

▼ HANGING IN MID-AIR How do you go about catching a trout that's hanging almost as if in mid-air in a small pool fed by a tiny waterfall? In the heat of the day, the fish aren't particularly hungry, merely killing time, milling around their watercourse. From what I've seen, only something dramatically different will attract their attention and stand any chance of working. Try pulling a big, dry fly across the surface, for example, or working a large nymph across a patch of exposed sand.

The United States

I've met a good number of top-class Irish guides and discussed the best ways to catch Irish fish. These men guide many nationalities and, when asked who are the real experts, they almost invariably say the North Americans. Certainly this is the case when they discuss moving water: they're more dubious about the US approach to lake fly fishing, but maybe that's because comparatively little takes place. Why are the Americans so good? Well, they certainly have the gear, but perhaps it's because their experience is so encompassing. Think of the challenge thrown out by those crystal streams of Montana. Then there's the salmon fishing for both Pacifics and Atlantics, as well as Dolly Vardens and many different types of trout. Then there's the challenge of black bass. My own experience of Americans has been shaped by bone-fishing experiences where I've found their ability to focus on almost invisible fish in clear water superlative.

◀ FISHING BY NUMBERS I have to record here one of the most bizarre fishing situations I've ever experienced with a fly rod. This water is just outside New York and I was filling in a few hours before catching a plane. All the anglers are allocated a number and you go to your own particular few feet of river. You have a look and if you're not happy with what you see, then the fishery's officers will pile in a few more trout for you to catch. You have an allotted catch limit and an allotted time span but, unless you prove to be an absolutely incompetent angler, you'll have reached your catch limit and be off the water virtually in minutes. It does, however, have the advantage of being crystal clear!

Scandinavia

Denmark, Sweden, Norway, Finland and Lapland offer some of the world's most dramatic clear-water fly-fishing opportunities. Once again, the scale of experience is very wide: fly fishing on one of the gushing Norwegian rivers is very different indeed to stalking a char on a high-altitude, heavily forested lake. Infrastructure is limited, and most of the Scandinavians I know accept a long, arduous hike as part of the day's fishing. They travel light and rapidly, and fish intensively when they arrive. Daylight hours for them are frequently flexible – in mid-summer it might remain light, or pretty much so, throughout the night, and you don't find Scandinavian fly fishermen tied by office hours.

▶ **The Right Way to Fish** When water is as clear as this – and could it get clearer? – a long line is often the only way to get to fish that would otherwise be spooked by the slightest movement. Note also how the angler is half-crouched, trying to lessen his impact on the surroundings – does this really make any difference? Well, speaking as a diver, virtually everything ill-considered and indiscreet on the river-bank is suicidal in clear-water conditions and when the weather is bright.

▶ **A Perfect Scenario** When the sunlight is bright on a crystal lake, every single knot, barb or anything else becomes glaringly obvious. Moreover, the trout have no inclination to feed. The perfect conditions will come later in the day, just as the sun is beginning to set and the light values are shrinking. Furthermore, if the evening breeze ripples the surface then your chances rise noticeably. This angler has opted to fish from a jetty. A boat would, however, be preferable because it provides more mobility. If you are without one, though, prepare to travel light and keep on the move, looking for feeding fish.

CHALK STREAM IN SUMMER

Summer, bright light, crystal-clear water and wary fish – the ingredients of a chalk-stream summer. This is some of the most challenging fishing to face the fly angler, particularly on catch-and-release waters where the trout learn rapidly from their mistakes. Even the appearance of the luscious mayfly can't guarantee success, especially with larger fish which are able to detect any flaw in the angler's approach. A lot of anglers, from what I see from beneath, are scuppered before they even put the fly in the water – chalk streams are generally small waters and, as well as being clear, they have banks that transmit the slightest sound to the fish. Beware of boggy banks that tremble or gravel banks that crunch. Tread very slowly and carefully and move well back from the water-line. One hundred and fifty years ago, the Wessex chalk streams proved the inspiration behind so many of the innovations in entomology and fly design that we take for granted today. The first of the true 'angler entomologists' appeared in these parts – men like Marryat, Halford and Skues carried the study of insects upon which trout fed to new levels.

◀ A LITTLE PIECE OF HEAVEN A millpond on a hot summer's day can provide added oxygen and slightly lower water temperatures, which stimulate lethargic fish into feeding.

Mayfly Season

Until a few years ago, local experts could state almost exactly when the first mayflies would rise from the water. Now, with the gradual rise of world temperatures, the mayfly hatch is becoming harder to predict. It still happens, of course – 2001 saw the heaviest hatch in living memory. Certainly, the few days when the mayflies hatch bring whole valleys to life. It's a period of plenty for all. Swans gorge on them, hawks rise and stoop for the flying insects, while in the river, coarse fish and eels gulp down the nymphs and emerging duns. Toads feed on the bodies of spent flies in the margins, and bats and owls take over the aerial attack at dusk. As for the trout, there is arguably no fly that they feed on more lustfully; this is the moment when that impossible-to-catch five-pounder just might make a costly mistake.

▶ **SPENT FLIES** The biggest and most cautious trout will often look for flies as they lie dead or dying in eddies and in the slowest of water. Feeding here can be slow and calculated, and the trout are unlikely to make a mistake. It's wise to let an artificial become bogged down in the surface film, and then perhaps give it a very slight trembling twitch if a fish approaches.

▶ **RIDING THE STREAM** The moment the fly hits the surface is a very important one. Trout can see the imitation fly in the air, and the faint vibrations that radiate from its kiss-like collision with the water give the desired impression of life. Sometimes it pays to pull back on the fly just before it hits the river to increase this effect. Take great care to mend your line and avoid the current dragging the fly off course.

◀ SUB-SURFACE The fly angler needs to try and recreate the footprint pattern of a real insect as it moves in the surface film. This can be a real problem – seen from below, the artificial mayfly rarely comes close at all. One idea is to tie the imitation somewhat larger than the real flies in the hope of stimulating the trout into believing a particularly lush meal is drifting past.

◀ WHEN THE WIND BLOWS A breeze can work in the angler's favour. Firstly, it will probably slow down the mayfly hatch so that fish don't become gorged. Secondly, a slight ripple on the surface of the river helps mask the angler's leader. Thirdly, it doesn't even seem to matter too much if the fly blows over onto its back as here… the impression of a dead or dying insect, with the promise of an easy meal, can be created.

◀ A BIG BROWN You'll often find the biggest fish in calm waters. The surface is less ruffled and it proves harder for insects to break free from the surface tension. The wary fish know instinctively that, in water such as this, feeding will be easier and they will have more time to inspect their prey. Take your time and watch all slow-moving stretches long and hard – the movement of the biggest fish will be slow and determined.

On the River-Bank

The world over, a chalk stream is an abundant source of life to all sorts of creatures, which work together to create a perfectly ordered aquatic environment. In an ideal world, everything plays its part and deserves its place. Even the large female pike, for example, shouldn't necessarily be persecuted, as she will eat vast numbers of young pike and keep down the destructive jack population; remove her from the environment and you're likely to find an explosion of tiny, snapping pike that really create havoc with trout stocks. The real threat to a delicate environment, such as a chalk stream, is when destructive aliens that weren't designed for this particular habitat are introduced. Mink are a perfect example, and so, too, are imported crayfish, which are having disastrous effects on indigenous crays and huge numbers of immature fish.

▶ **HEAD OF THE FOOD CHAIN** Otters are a sure sign of the health of a river and should be encouraged. You may fear that they will prey upon precious stocks of brown trout but, in truth, they're more likely to search out a sluggish pike like this one or burrow into the mud for eels. Otters also range on land for food; in the breeding season they prey heavily on local rabbit populations.

▶ **WATER VOLES** The existence of the charming water vole along the river-banks suggests good river management. Its presence indicates that reed beds are being managed sensitively and, vitally, that the rapacious mink is being kept under strict control – something beneficial to all forms of wildlife. Good river management is not simply to do with fishing alone – the modern view is that the entire ecosystem must be protected.

Nymph Fishing

To become anything like an expert at nymph fishing, you really should take time out and watch how nymphs actually work in the water so that you can imitate them to a fairly passable degree at least. Fly fishing is really natural history in action, and time spent watching the burrowing of the caddis is certainly time well spent. Also, look very carefully at how your nymphs work in the water. Do they look natural? How can you work them to best effect? The other major consideration is the river itself. Rivers have an almost magical life of their own. You don't need to be a diver to experience what I'm talking about: choose a warm day on a shallow, safe water and just let yourself drift along with it, preferably with a friend there for a bit of added security. You'll soon see how intricate and complex the currents are. If you begin to think of the river as a three-dimensional piece of water, your nymph presentation will soon take on extra life.

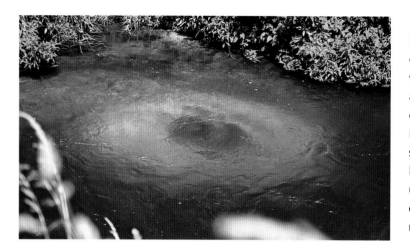

◀ **THE VAGARIES OF THE CURRENT**
I spent some time lying in the centre of this mini-whirlpool, which was about five feet deep at its core. The variation of the current was astounding, as was its power for such a small stream, so there's an important lesson for the nymph fisher – understanding the currents will enable you to present your nymph in the most natural way.

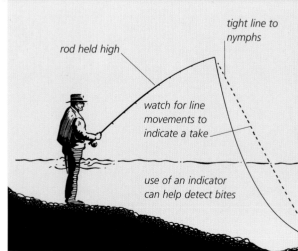

rod held high

tight line to nymphs

watch for line movements to indicate a take

use of an indicator can help detect bites

Nymph Fishing

Nymph fishing is an art form: you have to choose the right pattern, fish it at the right depth, in the right place, and at the right speed to a taking fish. You also have to detect the take, which can be very gentle. Polaroid glasses will help you see as much as possible of the action. You can strike on a hunch... perhaps the white gash of a mouth opening or the trout unexpectedly moving from its lie in the water. Keep very close contact with your nymph, so you have a focused idea of where it's operating, and make sure the nymph drifts as naturally as possible down to the waiting fish.

▶ **THE GRAVEL BED** Presenting a nymph in quick, clear, relatively shallow water is a difficult skill to master. The trout can see everything clearly, especially the line as it lands. Also, the fast upper layer of water is likely to skate the line, pulling the fly unnaturally fast over the gravel bed. Watch the water carefully before making your approach. Use cover on the bank to get as close as possible, as the less line you have out the better.

▶ **UPSTREAM NYMPHING** Upstream nymphing in skinny, clear water like this gives you the best chance of presenting the fly without undue drag. Short, precise casts remove the danger of placing the heavy fly line itself over a skittish fish. Wade very quietly and try to keep a weed bed between you and the fish you are targeting. Be aware of the sun and the lie of your shadow.

▶ **EAGLE EYES** In clear water and decent light, this lovely brown trout moved to intercept a small nymph from at least three feet away, which reinforces my belief that their eyesight is extremely keen. Therefore, you need to think very carefully about how you can disguise your line and leader in weed, riffles or anything that breaks their outline. Do not rush your time on the water.

ON THE SURFACE

Without a shadow of doubt, the finest bit of dry-fly fishing I've ever been fortunate enough to witness was on a Wessex river some fifteen years ago. Dermot Wilson was the angler in question and, as the sun set, he became galvanized, a man transformed into a heron, an assassin in the dusk. I'd flogged the water throughout the daylight hours and caught next to nothing. Dermot fished for those last precious twenty twilight minutes and caught three fine wild brown trout. I felt humbled – 'No need', he told me, 'it's simply this: fishing on the surface for educated fish in clear water is one of the most difficult, stringent tasks any game angler can set himself. If you are forced into this position, simply wait until the light is at its lowest and then at least you stand some sort of chance'. Fifteen years later, I can now see what Dermot meant. Lying on the bed of a shallow, clear river looking up at a fly, leader and trout line, it's almost impossible to understand why any fish should make such a mistake as to fall for it.

▲ LINE OFF THE WATER In the vast majority of situations it's quite impossible to keep your tippet off the water's surface, but if you're fishing close enough to do so, believe me, it will serve you well.

The Rising Trout

It's usual to associate a trout with its lie and to some degree this is correct. However, it's important to extend the concept of what a lie actually means. Yes, trout are territorial, but rather than having a simple, restricted lie, they're much more likely to have a patrol route. Trout rely on food coming down the current towards them, that drift of insects that spells breakfast, lunch and supper. They know where that drift will be at its most healthy at any given point of the day, and they will act to benefit from it. So, for example, as the day dies, you might well find trout in quicker, thinner water where there is an abundance of insects. In the heat of the day, you might find trout deeper or sheltering under weed, picking off food items that feel, quite erroneously, safe there.

It's important to realize that trout are masters of their environment, always on the prowl, always eager to investigate anything within their line of vision that looks remotely edible. The key to all this is to study the water in minute detail. If you see a good trout rise, don't dash in, but wait and watch. The more you build up a picture of its movements, the more likely you are to present the fly at exactly the right time and in exactly the right place. As Dermot said to me that night he went to work with such deadly efficiency, 'It's all about controlled impatience'.

▶ **CATCHING THE DRIFT**
Traditionally, a dry fly is cast upstream to meander its way towards a rising trout. This mimics food in the drift. There are times, however, when it pays to just twitch it against the current, or to even lift it out of the water completely for an instant; trout will react to this or any other sign of life.

Emerger Patterns

These are designed to imitate that stage of an aquatic insect's life when it is actually emerging right on the surface of the water. While the emerger is trapped on the surface, in the film of water, its struggles attract a trout, which realizes that this particular food form is virtually defenceless. Fishing an emerger successfully calls for very delicate presentation.

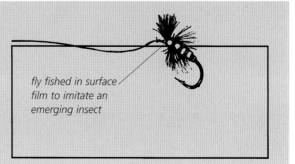

fly fished in surface film to imitate an emerging insect

▲ **MOVING IN FOR A CLOSE LOOK** Trout are great inspectors of foods and will often come as close as an inch or two before turning away, especially in slower water, where the current gives them more time to discriminate. In quicker, thinner water, a trout may be hurried into a mistake. In deeper water, where sight fishing is impossible, an angler might well have scores of inspections for every single take, and chances are that when the take does come, it's so gentle as to be missed time and time again.

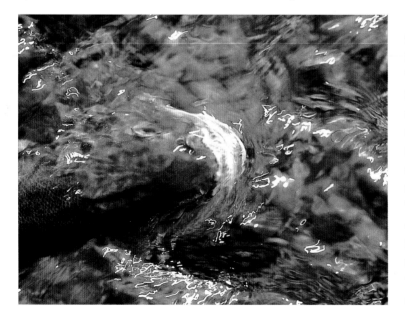

◀ **TAKING THE FLY** There are times when you can feel totally battered and bruised by defeat. The trout appear to be just too well-educated to make a mistake on a bright day in clear water. Nothing seems to succeed. Then again, there are certain things in your favour, such as this gratifying sight. That flash of white as the trout opens its mouth and sips in an insect is the perfect giveaway – especially for the nymph fisherman, who will use it as a signal to strike.

Sipped In

When I was a teenager, it was the work of two master fly anglers, Brian Clarke and John Goddard, that first alerted me to the fact that trout take different food items in a variety of different ways. Indeed, if you're unsure what type of fly to present, watch how the fish is feeding, as this will present a wealth of clues. Once again, it's important to take your time and really study the water in front of you, and I don't mean a cursory glance – I'm talking about a hawk-like, penetrative study. Watch an individual fish for perhaps half a day, and see how it takes a sedge or a free-swimming shrimp, or digs for a caddis that it's spotted emerging from beneath a rock. The trout can be fat and lazy or wiry and athletic, but the body language of the moment can show precisely what it's feeding upon.

▶ **FISHING IN THE SURFACE FILM** When a trout is feeding but its mouth does not break surface, then it is hunting small insects trapped within the surface film or trying to break through it. To see what's happening, watch very closely indeed, and even use a pair of binoculars. This is the time when a fly hanging from the surface film, as seen here, is likely to be taken.

▶ **GIVING AUDIBLE CLUES** Sound, too, is an important indicator. Suppose you hear a kissing or sipping noise with very little surface displacement, then, in all probability, you're looking at a slow-moving fish browsing off dead or dying insects. If the current isn't pulling your dry fly off course, then there's nothing wrong at this stage in leaving it as long as you can. Give your fly the odd twitch as a trout approaches to give it those tantalizing indications of a faltering life.

What the Trout Sees

Until trout learn to talk, no diver or angler will know exactly what they see, what they think or why they decide to take or reject an artificial fly. I believe that in clear, bright water the eyesight of the trout is pretty well unfailing. However, a light ripple on the surface or the shade thrown by a tree's branches or the dappling effect of weed can diffuse that eagle-eyed focus to a fractional, but very important, degree. Again, thinking back to Dermot, fish are undoubtedly often caught at dusk simply because there are a lot of flies hatching at that time and the trout are very busy, but it's also because there's less light to pinpoint the angler's tackle and highlight our hideous mistakes.

◀ **UNABLE TO RESIST** Small trout can behave in quite a mad way, chasing all sorts of food items and doing all manner of things that are not really wise for survival. Big trout such as this one, however, are totally different creatures, and they rarely, if ever, do anything that's out of character. It takes a really appetizing food item to make them behave irrationally, and during the mayfly season they do just this. The mayflies are just so big, so succulent that they are irresistible, and I was thrilled to see just how far away this trout spotted a gorgeous mouthful. Trout will certainly come eight to ten feet up or across the stream to intercept the mayfly – quite something when you think of all the clutter and oxygen bubbles in an average stretch of water.

◀ **A WORLD OF MOVEMENT** River water of any speed creates a world of motion. Flies working in the surface film can look wondrously realistic, not necessarily like any specific insect or creature but they just give the impression of a mysterious life form too juicy to ignore. This is where a fly scores over a spinner: a jinking piece of metal will always look a hard, unnatural thing compared with a well-tied fly.

▲ **IN THE PERFECT POSITION** Big trout move less and more slowly than small ones, picking their food items carefully. Spent or crippled flies are preferred, as they are largely trapped in the surface film from where they find it difficult to escape. Here we see an artificial mimicking just that situation. Look for areas where surface scum builds up: in lakes this will be in bays, while in rivers it may be in backwaters or eddies. The big trout know that there are pickings galore in these locations.

▶ **JUST TOO OBVIOUS** The problem in slower water is that the trout has much more chance to examine the fly carefully before coming to any decision. A hook bend glinting like this in the sunlight can be an absolute giveaway. Exactly the same problem exists in all styles of fishing, whether fly, bait or lure. Camouflaged hooks may be the answer, or flies tied with the hook above rather than below.

▲ **IN FADING LIGHT** Every trout angler fishing a large lake anywhere in the world dreads the still, bright, steaming days of high summer, especially when a breeze is blowing. What can be done? Well, you can dig the depths with a fast-sinking line or you can pray for cloud to blanket the sun. Alternatively, wait until dusk, as did my friend, Johnny Jensen, seen here justifiably proud of a huge, wild, Irish brown.

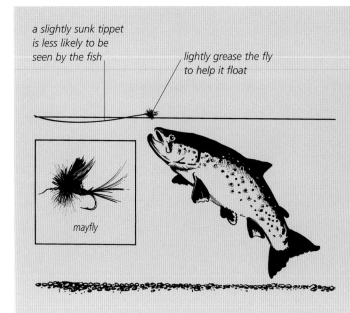

a slightly sunk tippet is less likely to be seen by the fish

lightly grease the fly to help it float

mayfly

Dry Flies

Keep false casts to a minimum because your prey is near the surface and is likely to see the line and leader over its head. If you're going to make a mistake, fall short rather than long, as this is less disruptive. Watch the fish before casting: most of them have a recognizable rhythm and you can predict when they are next likely to rise. Don't cast at the water, but above it: aim a foot or so above the surface and you'll find the fly drops more gently. Avoid drag and try to impart a bit of wiggle in your line to allow the fly to drift over the fish as naturally as possible.

BODY LANGUAGE

All fish species speak strong body languages, but this is especially the case among the salmonids. Wild fish are invariably the quickest of all to react to changes, and they are more wary and more easily stressed when their carefully worked out lifestyles are challenged. Most experienced fishermen recognize the most basic forms of body language – for example, when a trout is either hungry and actively finning the current looking for food or when it is much more relaxed, holding its position on the bottom and rarely bothering to intercept or investigate any passing food item. Other changes are more subtle and are often more difficult to read. All manner of occurrences can affect a trout's behaviour – bright sunlight, low water, rapid temperature change, the interference of man or the appearance of an otter or an osprey, for example.

▲ **FEEDING WITH CONFIDENCE** If you see a wild trout working keenly in shallow water, then you can guess it feels secure in its world. In theory, if you don't make mistakes, this is an eminently catchable fish.

Sulking Fish

Fish are very sensitive to their environment, and it doesn't take much to upset them, be it water temperature, currents or debris in the water. One thing that also plays a huge part in upsetting fish is, naturally, methods of catch and release. The arguments both for and against catch and release are massive. A general view is that special, large, wild fish should be released. When returning fish to the water there are certain vital rules to be followed to avoid producing a sulking fish that will be ever more aware of anglers. Barbless hooks make for quick, easy, painless unhooking. Try to keep the fish in the water while the unhooking process takes place. If you need to take a photograph, do it with the fish lifted just inches from the water and dunk it back in between each and every shot. When you release the fish, hold it gently against the current until it summons up the energy to move away. Ensure that your contact with the fish is minimal and is as gentle and unobtrusive as possible. Any fish bleeding from the gills is almost certain to die, so it's better to kill it and put it to good use in the kitchen.

◀ **UPON RELEASE** This is a small brown trout that was caught and released in a fairly uncaring sort of fashion. The photograph was taken between two and five minutes after capture. The fish is holding its own in the current but it is quite obviously distressed. The trout's skin is blotchy and its movements are erratic and jerky. The fish hasn't returned to its original lie and is drifting, looking for another area in which to settle.

▶ **STILL RECOVERING** This is the same fish half an hour after its release. The fish has now taken up physical sanctuary between an old brick and some waving water weed. It's wedged in uncomfortably, seeking out what current it can find and perhaps taking reassurance from the hiding-hole it's created for itself. In the event, it was two days before this particular trout returned to its original lie and began feeding again – a clear lesson that catch and release must be done properly.

▶ **OUT IN THE STORM** This trout is in some three or four feet of water and seems disturbed by the leaves that are going past it. It refuses to hold anything like a permanent situation, but is constantly moving backwards and forwards across the current looking for relief. Remember your trout is a living, thinking creature that will go to great lengths to make its life as comfortable as possible.

▶ **THE FLOOD** Nor do trout like sudden floods of cold water. I stumbled across this one in a millpond that was only just beginning to fine down and where visibility was still only minimal. It looked miserable and was wedged in among boulders along the bottom where it had obviously found sanctuary. Silt and fine sand had collected on it and it obviously wasn't in the mood for feeding.

▲ **FINING DOWN** Rivers are extremely volatile environments, especially in this day and age of less than sympathetic drainage engineering schemes. Rivers that do go up and down undoubtedly cause trout more discomfort than watercourses where everything is more gradual. A sudden flush of water can be beneficial, but anything more than this can put the trout off the feed for a while.

◀ **ODDITIES** Here is a trout that you might think was frightened. It is holed up behind rocks with just its tail poking out to the world. Maybe it was my presence or perhaps it had been caught before. Strangely, I found it three or four times in exactly the same place over a period of about ten days when diving. Salmon frequently behave in exactly this way when they're running upstream. Perhaps it's a means of security for certain fish when they're not actively feeding.

Unhooking Trout

Guide your fish – be it trout, salmon or sea trout – into shallow water where you can approach it without danger. Try not to use a net, and do not touch the fish any more than necessary, if at all. If the fly is not in the lips of the fish, use forceps to access a deep hook quickly and efficiently. Ensure that the fish is strong enough to cope before it moves out into the current – a fish washed away downriver on its back will drown.

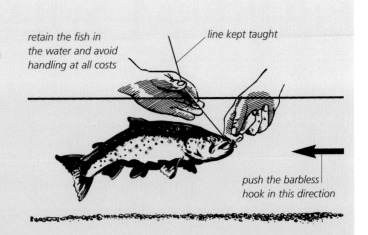

retain the fish in the water and avoid handling at all costs

line kept taught

push the barbless hook in this direction

▶ **UNCATCHABLE** These two trout pictured in clouded water seem quite oblivious to the angler. What's interesting is that they couldn't be bothered to get out of the way of something that should have alarmed them. We think of trout, rightly, as very wary creatures, perpetually looking for food opportunities or the threats of danger. However, there is another side to them – when conditions cause them to switch off they can be as comatose as any pike.

▶ **RESTING HAPPILY** I saw this trout in high summer in a twinkling chalk stream among curling weed, and, despite his lack of movement, there was nothing at all wrong with him. He was simply happy doing nothing. A fellow angler drifted a couple of flies past him and he budged not an inch. Fin movement was at a minimum and the body was hardly flexing at all against the current… as close to asleep as it's possible to get.

PROBLEM SOLVING

In the long-gone days when I used to teach and ran the school's angling club, I soon realized that the child who managed to do only seventy per cent of things right caught next to nothing. Once he upped his skills to the eighty-per cent mark, one or two fish began to be caught. When only ten per cent was being done obviously wrong, he'd catch quite a few fish, and with only five per cent of mistakes the success rate rose appreciably. This is the essence of fishing – presenting the right fly, in the right place, at the right time and with the maximum possible delicacy and realism. These skills are the bare bones of fly fishing, but you also need to push things just that little bit further if you're really going to achieve all you wish: imagination is an important part of this. If the traditional methods don't work, then go out on a limb – use a bit of lateral thinking, try something absolutely unexpected and the fish might well respond.

▲ THE CAUTIOUS BASS A large-mouth bass that finally took a fly. Bass will often investigate a fly over and over again before making a decision, so keep changing flies, keep casting, and a take could be yours.

Visible Problems

It's probable that the eyes of a salmonid can focus at both short and long distances and over a wide field of vision. Other considerations also affect sight – notably light, water clarity and the effect of currents and wind. Sometimes vision is impaired – say after a flood. Bright light also has its own effect: imagine what it does to the translucent feathers of a fly. Consider, too, that the fish's brain is probably not large enough to take in all the information that the eye passes to it: it will sift what it feels are the most important items but ignore others. So, there can be no hard and fast rules to your fishing: the reaction of each fish is always going to be different.

▶ **THE QUESTION OF FLASH** Light-coloured lines are obviously more visible from above the surface and can therefore indicate takes more clearly than dark ones can. The problem is that from under the surface light-coloured lines can give off a certain amount of flash in bright conditions. It's also important not to have loops in the fly line as they act as mirrors and send out extra warning signals. Bear in mind, then, that your tackle is not going to fool a salmonid if it doesn't look right or if it's presented badly.

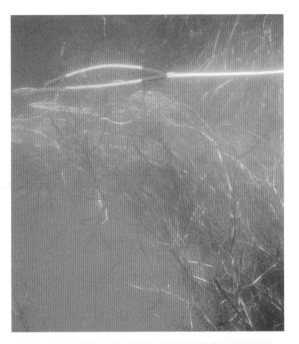

▶ **THE EFFECT OF SUNLIGHT** This shot was taken at around six feet deep on a bright, sunlit day. Just look how the light has caught the line and turned it into a dagger-like object, easily visible to all and sundry. To avoid this problem, try fishing in the shade of an overhanging tree or look for a deeper hole where the light is less intense or fish closer to weed beds where the line is less obvious.

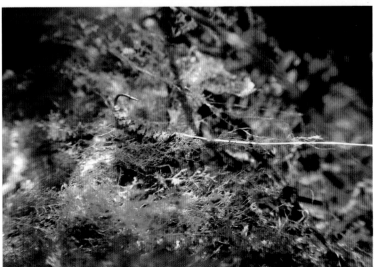

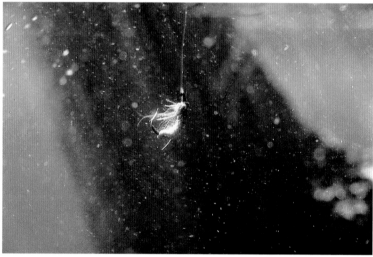

◀ **THE LOOP** A trout will frequently look kindly on a nymph worked very slowly indeed or even just allowed to sink to the bottom. Try, though, to maintain a direct contact to avoid your leader looping and becoming ever more obvious. Watch how your nymph and leader work and look in shallow clear water – does it need a dust shot a finger's length from the hook; will a different colour tippet help?

◀ **LINE STIFFNESS** Experimentation in the shallows or even at home in your bath can point out the material that suits your nymph to perfection. Lighter line is often more successful than thicker line. The thicker the line, the more stiff it will be and the less realistically the fly works. Today, a whole range of tippet materials are on the market, including fluorocarbons that can give softness along with very low diameter.

◀ **WEEDED** In rivers, especially, too few anglers appreciate how many particles of weed and rubbish are floating in the current. A nymph is frequently best fished on a dead drift but you can easily pick up clutter such as this, which will prove an immediate alarm signal. If suspended weed proves a problem, avoid the slack where weed builds up and find the quicker runs.

Positioning

Positioning your nymph is all-important. A nymph hanging suspended in open water rarely looks convincing, as this is not where the fish expect to find food. This is where structure comes in – try to get a good impression of the underwater terrain of any river or lake. For this you'll need Polaroids, a clear day and plenty of time. Look out for rocks, sunken branches, reeds, weed beds and all the sorts of places where nymphs and other aquatic food items are likely to be working. This is where you'll find the fish, too – not in open water where there's little cover and a restricted amount of food. Think very carefully, not just about how you are going to fish your fly but also where you're going to position it. Get a clear idea of how quickly your fly sinks, so you know when it's reached a certain level and a particular structure that you want to fish. Don't do anything blind and don't rely on guesswork; the clearer your plan, the greater your success.

▶ **SOLID STRUCTURE** Allowing a nymph to work on or around rocks or sunken branches closely simulates natural behaviour. Work the nymph very slowly to mimic the natural. At times, let it lie completely still, at rest. The slower your nymph is being worked, the gentler the take, so you need to watch very carefully for any unexpected movement on the leader. Tighten the moment you suspect a take.

▶ **BENEFICIAL WEED** Many anglers are wary of operating close to weed beds for fear of snagging tackle, but it's here that trout expect to find a great deal of food, and they'll feed comparatively unwarily. Your leader will also be masked by the weed and the light will be diffused. Don't work the fly too quickly or it will get caught up; the odd twitch will attract any trout's attention.

◀ **Left to Rest** It can be a good idea to allow the fly simply to rest in fairly sparse weed beds. The line to it is almost completely hidden but the trout won't have any problems in sighting a potential item of food. Twitch the fly occasionally, especially if you're sight fishing and can see a fish approaching.

◀ **Natural Habitats** Steve Thornton is an expert fly tier who creates flies that look as close to the natural as you're ever going to find. This large nymph is particularly heavily weighted so it can get right down to the bottom weed in the fastest flowing water. A quick current will always want to snatch at the leader and pull your fly off course, so fish as short a line as you can and, if possible, wade so that you can keep in a direct line.

◀ **A Cabbage Leaf** In water that's slow and clear enough, you can often latch your fly onto an underwater cabbage leaf such as this. Once again, the leader is nicely masked and you can virtually leave the fly static, perhaps just moving it if a fish approaches. Expect slow but confident takes.

Caddis, Shrimp and the Endless Larder

Most waters offer an almost endless variety of small aquatic insects for trout to feed upon. Many of these come to the fish in the drift of the river but trout, and all game fish, are very active diggers for food. They're explorers and exploiters, and it pays to get your nymph or shrimp right down into the sort of crevices where they're working. Don't be afraid of weed and snags: if you tie your own flies, financial losses will obviously be minimized. By casting a nymph upstream and letting it drop down along with the current you can achieve much greater fishing depths than by casting downstream and across. The problem with upstream nymphing – any nymphing come to that – is one of take recognition. Watch the leader minutely for any sign of a take and also keep an eye open for the sign of a turning fish in the area of your nymph.

▶ **THE CADDIS GRUB** Given the chance, trout and grayling will gorge upon caddis grubs, especially if they become separated from the safety of a case and become instantly vulnerable. Caddis grubs come in all shades – brown and buttery-yellow are common, but you'll frequently find varying shades of green. Begin, perhaps, with a white imitation, moving on to yellow and then green as a final attempt.

▶ **THE WORKING FLY** When I was taught the Czech nymph technique in Bohemia several years ago, it was impressed upon me that not all nymphs work properly. Franta, my coach and a member of the Czech fly-fishing team, would test each fly over and over in the water by his feet to ensure it looked right either in the drift or when it was moving along the bottom like this.

◄ **PERFECT MOVEMENT** It's hard to describe exactly what the perfect movement is, but the nymph shouldn't wobble from side to side but proceed in a balanced, positive way. How does the nymph sink? A heavy nymph should go down quick and true, but the flutter of a lighter one can be enticing. A great deal depends on the depth and speed of water that you are tackling. Consider every situation and choose the right nymph for the lie before you.

◄ **FINER LINE** Here you see what I mean about finer line being that little bit more flexible. Note how it coils over the stones rather than looking poker-like. How can you know, though, how your fly is acting deep in the water? Take time out, as Franta recommends, to experiment in the shallows where you can actually discover how to make your fly look as natural as possible.

Buzzers

The buzzer is the angler's name for several species of large, non-biting midges that hatch in the warmer months. You'll find large hatches in the mornings and evenings especially. Fish in the more sheltered bays where insect activity is intense and you will find it somewhat easier to pick up indications of a take. You can fish your buzzer virtually static or retrieve it with sharp, short pulls.

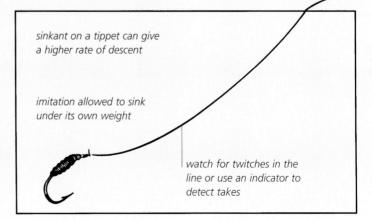

sinkant on a tippet can give a higher rate of descent

imitation allowed to sink under its own weight

watch for twitches in the line or use an indicator to detect takes

▶ **THE BUBBLE** A lot of small food items attract tiny air bubbles to them and, as we can see here, this makes the artificial look very natural indeed; it also enhances visibility. Choosing nymphs with just a few extra legs and whiskers can intensify the effect. Subtle changes of colour and texture can have a marked effect under water – hence the recent successes of the epoxy buzzer patterns, for example.

▶ **POSITIONING** Whether you're fishing in mid-water or on the bottom, sometimes the nymph adopts an unconvincing position. Of course, if you can't see your nymph, and you rarely can, you won't really know when this is happening. The answer is just to keep the nymph working and present it in as many different attitudes as possible, and maintain your concentration at a high level.

▶ **THE TAKE** Here the nymph is looking much more realistic, but, however it is lying, the great art of nymph fishing lies in detecting the take and striking. My own observations are that up to ninety per cent of takes are completely undetected from the river-bank, so fish tight, close and focused. Keep a portion of your leader visible on the surface, and, if need be, a strike indicator can be useful in rough conditions or low light.

Off the Top

We've already stressed how fish love hunting in the surface film because that is where so many dead and dying insects are trapped. Always remember that the more slowly the water is moving, the more time the fish has to inspect your fly and decide whether or not to take it. On the surface light values are more enhanced as well, so presentation has to be even more carefully thought out. Seeing takes, however, is easier when fishing on the surface than when fishing deep down, and fewer fish are going to be missed.

▲ **PERFECT FOCUS** This was an interesting take. This big fish had already refused several flies worked slowly past it, but when a big streamer was whacked over its head and then pulled back fast enough to cause a wake, it just couldn't refuse. The fish is utterly focused on the fly.

◀ **STRANGE TO BEHOLD** Looked at from the fish's point of view, a lure near the surface imitates virtually everything… certainly a small fish scurrying about its business. It's blindingly obvious why flies tend to outfish spinners: the softness of the materials allows the fly to sway in the current, to look alive and, importantly, to collect those tell-tale air bubbles.

The Real and the Artificial

When we tie and present our flies we are looking for creations that are close enough to the real thing to trigger a feeding reaction. Colour, shape, movement... these are the characteristics that we are hoping to imitate, so it is important to learn about the insects on which trout and other game fish feed. Time spent studying various insects is central, and a little knowledge in this respect makes choosing a fly from the box so much easier. Learn to identify flies by superficial characteristics – shape, size and colour particularly. Begin to distinguish up-wing flies, such as mayflies and olives, from the roof-shaped wing flies, notably sedges and caddis. You also have the flat-winged flies, such as midges, gnats and buzzers. Then there's a wide variety of aquatic and territorial insects. Add to that beetles, snails, leeches, grasshoppers and moths, and you will begin to realize what a wide variety of food forms there is to imitate. Let's take a sea trout: it's a pitch-black night but it can still make out your sparsely dressed fly tied to a size ten; suddenly it takes and the battle is on. Does it actually think it's eaten any specific type of food or has your fly simply engaged its interest by its shape and its movement? Fish are not professors of entomology but creatures earning their living.

▶ **WATCH THE BEETLE** It was Brian Clarke years ago who stressed the importance of watching food items in their natural habitat to gain a better understanding of how they move. This is one of the most important pieces of knowledge when it comes to imitating their movements with your artificial.

▶ **TRIGGERS** This artificial fly doesn't look like anything in particular and the hook is particularly ungainly, but there are enough similarities with a beetle to trigger at least a less well-educated trout into a take. Movement is an important key – hold it in the surface film and then let it sink near-vertically just like the real beetle itself.

◀ **POSITIONING AGAIN** Watching aquatic creatures in their own environment provides valuable lessons. Water beetles, for example, spend a lot of time resting on underwater twigs and branches. They'll stay there, quite immobile, for several minutes before moving back to the surface to take in air. This provides an obvious pointer to the areas in which you should work a beetle imitation.

◀ **CATCHING THE LIGHT** Prey fish will spend much of their time trying to be as inconspicuous as possible, but this small shoal of sticklebacks is working in open water. Look how the sun has picked out one unfortunate as the most likely target. It can obviously pay to choose a fly with a bit of flash to it.

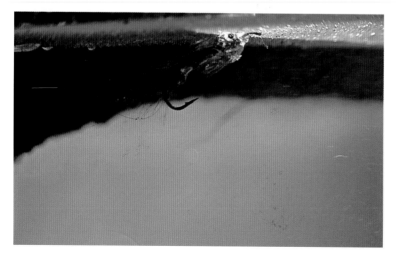

◀ **IMITATING LIFE** See how the head of this fly is catching the light and shining, just as brightness reflects off the sides of the real fish in the photo above. Make sure you impart movement to the fly – a number of tiny twitches can make an imitation look like a tired or wounded fish.

▶ **KEEPING IN THE SHADE** This stickleback is behaving typically. It has picked a gloomy piece of water and is hanging immobile close to a branch. When it does decide to move, it will be in quick, short, erratic bursts followed by long periods hanging motionless in mid-water, fins fanning rapidly.

▶ **IMITATIVE FLY** This fly may not look exactly like a stickleback, but in profile and positioning it does a good enough job. Using our knowledge of how the natural stickleback operates, the answer for the angler is six-inch retrieves followed by thirty-second pauses.

▶ **FLUID MOTION** Any fly that's intended to imitate a small fish must have fluidity and work with the current like a living creature. Try and work flies in the areas that small fish habitually use – slacks, areas sheltered by branches and weed beds. Watch for signs of trout feeding on fry in the shallows and react quickly.

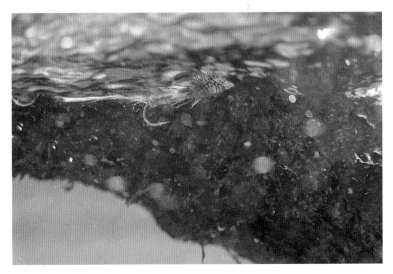

◀ **UNEXPECTED FOOD** When you study small food items closely, you will come across the unexpected – flies perhaps yet to be devised! While I haven't seen trout get particularly excited over tadpoles, I've seen very young newts such as this being consumed eagerly in early spring on two occasions – is there a fly pattern out there?

◀ **DELICACY** Many of the trout's favourite food items show extraordinary delicacy in the water and, once again, they are highlighted with trapped air bubbles. They move very slowly indeed as though suspended in space. Many of these small insects are taken as they rise gently to the surface, so retrieve as slowly as you can.

◀ **GENERAL IMITATION** This small buzzer shows a fair imitation of the natural, but by suspending it just under the surface, barely moving, you're imitating many a small insect, not just a fly soon to hatch. Looking at this photograph and the one above, remember that sparse dressing can often be an advantage. A nearly bare hook can be more suggestive of life than an over-fussy imitation.

▲ **THE DEAD FLY** You don't necessarily have to move a fly at all to make it an attractive food item. A large part of a fish's time is spent searching the bottom looking for edible items that can be picked up with the minimum of effort. A tiny shot close to the fly can keep the line pinned on to the sand or gravel and stop it looping up.

▶ **DEEP DARK WATER** Much of what I've seen and described here has involved shallow, relatively clear water. I'm aware that deep, dark water can provide different problems, demanding different solutions. However, even many feet down, light and movement are still important considerations, as the clarity of this shot demonstrates. Always work your flies with care and thought, whatever the depth you are fishing.

The World of Light

Light is very important, both above and below the water. Light at times can ruin our chances by highlighting leader material or flashing off the tip of a hook. Equally, it can trigger success – the shaft of light off a goldhead nymph, for example, can look tantalizingly like an oxygen bubble. The new epoxy buzzers look fantastically realistic when the light hits them at certain angles during certain movements. So, light can be both a friend and an enemy to the fly fisherman. It is true that the hot, still days on a pond-like lake are generally seen as the kiss of death, but if you can find a quickly-flowing stream nearby then things can be quite different. Equally, if you're on the coast, you'll find that light seems to stimulate the mackerel shoals into exaggerated feeding. Dawn and dusk are the preferred times for most forms of fly fishing – along with true night for the sea-trout angler – but it doesn't do to be too inflexible.

◀ **DOWN DEEP** This photograph was taken in water that was quite deep and none too clear, but on a very sunny day. Note how this trout is picked out by the sunlight even far from the surface. Leaders and lines in these conditions do look obvious, and cloudy, windy days can prove much more successful for obvious reasons.

◀ **A SPARKLER** There are exceptions, though. This trout, which had been digging in sand and gravel for insects, is obviously attracted by a fly suddenly struck by rays of light. The fish didn't take – probably my presence put the fish off – but it did signal interest for some seconds. By the way, never underestimate how energetically trout will dig for food.

TROUT CONSERVATION

If wild trout are present in a healthy, sparkling river, not only are they beautiful to look at, fascinating to study and a joy to catch, but they are also a reflection of how we are treating that particular environment.

We've already talked about catch and release and its important role in preserving numbers of pristine fish… providing it's done correctly; just as important is the role played by fishermen in water management. In developed countries particularly, rivers suffered monumentally throughout the eighteenth, nineteenth and twentieth centuries. Pollution, water abstraction, industrial and agricultural run-off, dredging and general neglect resulted in a sharp decline of naturally-breeding trout. Today there are a growing number of anglers that want not just to catch wild fish but, much more importantly, want to create waters that are friendly towards them. There's more technology, more knowledge and perhaps more will than ever before.

▲ **GENTLY DOES IT** Without even using a landing net, you can simply draw your fish into the shallows, hold the hook, give it a twist and the barbless hook should come clear instantly.

Guardians of the Stream

I've worked with naturalists for long enough to know that the majority of them are only interested in the aquatic environment in the most sketchy of ways. Certainly, they're not very concerned with fish or with anything that operates totally beneath the surface film. There is, as we all know, a huge amount of interest in otters, kingfishers, newts, toads and water voles. Anything that operates within our sight is cherished and protected, but fish aren't like that. The majority of the fish's life is carried on in secret and is unguessed at by the majority of the public. This is where fishermen come in: anglers love fish and will work hard to protect them. Catching fish is important to anglers, admittedly, but so, too, is their environment and welfare. There are many arguments in support of angling but this is the main one: take angling away from most aquatic environments and these fragile habitats would be very much the poorer for it.

▲ **At Work** After repeated floods, an important spawning redd on this little chalk stream has become clogged with silt. The stream's guardians have arrived, complete with boat and a pumping mechanism, which serves as a type of mobile vacuum cleaner on the river bed. This vital work is carried out in the summer so that the river can settle well before the back end of the season when the trout begin to spawn. By then, all the impact of the work has subsided and the gravels are colonized with rich insect life.

▶ **THE PROBLEM** Here we can see a close-up of the composition of the redd. The gravel and stones can be seen clearly, but the redd has become clogged up with a grey, clinging mud. This means that the trout can't cut the redd successfully and lay their eggs down deep. Also, the texture precludes oxygen getting to the eggs in necessary quantities. Nor is the mix productive for fly life, so the river suffers doubly.

▶ **GETTING RID OF THE SILT** Up close, you can see the work in progress. Look behind the three men and their canine friend and you can see the clouds of silt drifting off downstream as the poisonous cloak is removed. Nature is wonderfully hardy and, given a helping hand, can recover very quickly. Modern techniques and approaches are really making the return of wild fish ever more possible on many waters.

▶ **POLISHED** Here is a handful of the redd after the work has been completed. The stones now glisten and they are no longer glued together. Consider how easily a trout can now make a cut for its eggs and how well they'll be oxygenated when laid. The fry will also find it much easier to get in among stones like these when they hatch, and a flood is less likely to dislodge them.

▲ **LATE AUTUMN** The work has been finished, the water has settled, but you can still see the glowing patches of cleaned redd resplendent after the renovation that's been carried out on them. There's enough ground here for several trout to spawn and for their fry to re-populate the river naturally. There is still work to be done of course: the banks will need to be maintained and new trees will be planted and encouraged to overhang the river.

◀ **HERE THEY COME** The trout come to investigate the redds that have been so carefully and lovingly prepared for them. Many fisheries are working very hard now at enlightened management. This can be very costly and is certainly time-consuming, but the wild fish that are encouraged to reproduce in this way are far more desirable then those from a fish farm.

GRAYLING METHODS

Fortunately, the days of grayling being reviled are rapidly slipping into the past. Grayling are one of the most fascinating of all our fly-caught species. They're beautiful, hard-fighting and tremendously obliging – happy to feed in the heat of the summer and in the coldest depths of winter. They're also highly demanding: because they are shoal fish, their defences are multiplied many fold and it's much more difficult to creep up on a shoal of grayling than it is on a single, solitary trout. Being a good trout fisherman doesn't automatically help when it comes to grayling: you'll find that grayling occupy different lengths of the river – another good reason for saying they don't compete with trout in most environments. Furthermore, grayling can be much more discriminating than trout when it comes to taking the artificial. A big grayling in

clear water, especially, will refuse virtually every fly in the box, and if it does take the very last one, the take is likely to be so gentle that well over ninety per cent are missed. Grayling are never spread through a river like currants in a cake, and it's very important for the angler to remain mobile and search large areas of water to locate them. You will rarely see them rise, but look for them down deep in slower pools where they might just look like pieces of sunken branch.

◀ **A LESSON IN CONCENTRATION** My great friend, Leo, the Dutch fly-fishing captain, fishes for grayling in a deep swirling slack. Note the short line and use of the leveller.

The Leveller

There are those trout fishermen who think that a leveller, a strike indicator, a float, or whatever you like to call it, is unsporting. This could well be the case in trout-fishing circles but when it comes to grayling, believe me, you will catch twenty grayling on the leveller for every single one that you catch without. The reason? Quite simply, a grayling can sip in and spit out an artificial in the blink of an eye, far more quickly than a trout can, so immediate observation of a take is essential. A second use of the leveller is implicit in its very name. Grayling generally feed at very specific depths and what the leveller does is keep your suspended nymph in line with the fish. Without a leveller, your nymph will simply plummet past the fish and hit bottom; some fish might stoop to take it, but you'd be missing the prime of the shoal. Experiment with setting the leveller at different depths until you find the critical taking point.

◀ **RIDING THE SURFACE** Choose your leveller carefully: it should be obvious to the eye, ride the stream elegantly, be buoyant enough to carry the nymph at the required depth and not be dragged under by every weed frond, and yet be forgiving enough to dip to the most tentative of grayling takes. Its shape can also be important – use a slim leveller for placid water and a more rounded design for rougher streams.

◀ **TO STRIKE OR NOT?** The leveller has dipped fractionally under the surface. There's a bit of an obstruction on the bottom – ideally, you'll be working your nymph or nymphs quite close to the bottom – so it's an agonizing decision. Strike unnecessarily and the very action is likely to disturb the shoal; delay it too long and the take is missed.

▶ **Burying** You're in no doubt when the leveller goes down as deeply as this. However, be warned – it doesn't happen often. Watch out, too, for the leveller just holding up in the current for a second, no more – this, too, means that a grayling has sucked the nymph in. Very occasionally, if you're very lucky, the leveller will actually move upstream a fraction – a dead give-away as the grayling seizes a nymph and moves back to its position.

▶ **Autumn and Winter Grayling** The great advantage of grayling is that you can fish for them during the cold months. However, there's often a severe leaf fall coating the river bottom. This is where a leveller really does come into its own – you can set it so that the nymph rides just clear of the offending vegetation. This leveller is set a fraction too deep, but a couple of trial runs and you'll soon be able to gauge the depth perfectly and run the nymph through just above bottom without catching the leaf stems.

Czech Nymphing

One of the basics of this technique is presenting a team of two or even three nymphs close to the river bed and making them work in as natural a way as possible. One heavy nymph will keep the team down in the critical area while the lighter ones will skip and work up to a foot from the bottom. Sensing the take is critical to any nymphing technique, so use your powers of touch and sight to their utmost.

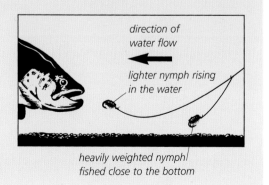

direction of water flow

lighter nymph rising in the water

heavily weighted nymph fished close to the bottom

Crystal Streams

Grayling fishing and crystal-clear water generally go hand in hand – the species just isn't happy in waters that are warm, murky or not sufficiently well oxygenated. Grayling, for these reasons, flourish from Alaska to Mongolia to the chalk streams of southern England. One of my happiest memories of this most visible form of fishing is in England's Derbyshire Dales, on the River Dove; I remember a particular pool that was so clear the grayling could be seen clearly at a depth of some fourteen or fifteen feet. It was hugely difficult to gauge exactly how deep the fish were lying and at what level they were feeding. Getting the fly a couple of feet over or under depth would ruin all chances of success. The fish were literally at my rod tip but, over the years, proved more frustratingly difficult to catch than almost any other fish that I can remember.

◀ **WADING** To get the very best out of your grayling fishing it pays to get as close to the grayling as possible, so that you can fish really tight and present the fly with maximum accuracy and delicacy. There's nothing about good grayling fishing that is sloppy or left to chance. The closer you can get to the fish without disturbing them and the shorter the line you're using the more immediate will be the strike to the most hesitant of takes.

◀ **KEEP ON THE MOVE** Rob Olsen, the illustrator for this book, holds a magnificent Mongolian grayling. Rob likes to be mobile and not stay at one piece of water for too long, which makes him the perfect grayling angler. Grayling tend to shoal up in small groups, so take three or four fish and then move on, constantly searching new pieces of water.

▶ **TRAINING THE EYE** Look carefully and you can just spot the fish. This is often all the experienced grayling angler sees – a mere suggestion of a shape, different colour and texture, a slight blurring of the bottom. Learning to spot grayling takes practice. Don't concentrate too much on any piece of water, but let your eye glaze somewhat, go slightly out of focus and often you'll almost subconsciously begin to pick up the presence of these mysterious fish.

▶ **SUCCESS** This grayling sipped in my friend's fly just as he was lifting it off the bottom and past its nose. The grayling thought the fly was about to escape, so it hit in a hurry and was well hooked; most grayling won't be. Often, you'll find them only attached by the merest sliver of skin, so go very lightly in the fight. Take your time, and if one should jump, lower your rod tip to decrease the pressure on the hook hold.

▶ **IN THE STREAM** Be careful if a grayling gets across the current and lifts its fin. The pressure of the water can pull the fish downriver and out of your control. Instead, as this photograph shows, bully the head of the grayling into the current and keep it coming all the way to the net.

ROAD TO THE ISLES

A fly rod is the key to a door that opens out onto the most magnificent of aquatic worlds. Fly gear is wondrous: a rod, a reel, a few spools of leader material, a box or two of flies and, with a combined weight of just a couple of pounds, you're free to travel the world. There's barely a single country that doesn't possess fish catchable on the fly. Indeed, there's barely a fish anywhere that can't be fly-caught.

Scotland itself is a remote and magical place: its ring of islands is even more so. North Uist was my destination for these shots – cloud-covered and remote, but offering thrilling opportunities for salmon, sea trout and brown trout, and sea fish such as bass and wrasse. A long and difficult journey indeed, but well worth it to see those rugged coastlines, the romantic rolling hills, the rushing rivers and beguiling lochs – not to mention welcoming generous people, quiet roads and the friendliest of pubs at night.

▲ **WATERS OF PROMISE** In the Isles, the heavily indented coastline means the sea is always close, both physically and psychologically. Salmon, sea trout and bass all move between fresh water and salt water, and the brackish pools are home to large predatorial browns.

Wild Waters

If you've learnt the art of fly fishing on a commercial fishery, a wilder water offering virgin fish takes some getting used to. In all probability, you will need to be up early and stay out late. You must also be prepared for long, sometimes hard, walks. Nor will there be neatly-designed casting platforms. Most of the time you'll be on your own, often contending with fierce winds. For this reason alone, it's useful to travel with gear rated up a notch or two on what you generally use. If you're used to smaller man-made fisheries, it's easy to feel daunted by these much large waters – don't be. Take local advice: fish each yard of water in front of you carefully and with confidence, and fish will soon appear. Learn to watch for signs: for example, if seals are working close in, the chances are there's a run of bass. If gulls are swooping down, perhaps it's because sea trout are forcing sand eels towards the surface. Out here in the wilds, everything happens for a reason and you'll soon begin to make the connections.

▶ **THE LAND OF TIDES** The flight into North Uist is revealing. You'll see a world that is more water than land and you begin to realize its incredible fishing opportunities. However, this is a world of water that is never still, always volatile, always challenging. Local knowledge is absolutely vital. It takes years of experience to build up a picture of the tides and of how and when the fish move with them. Rainfall, too, is very important, swelling the spawning streams from the lochs into the smaller lakes, or lochans, and into the final redds of the salmon and sea trout. There are many fish present here, but they work within a complex system that takes time to unravel.

Silver from the Sea

There's no more glamorous a species than the sea trout, but they've had a very hard time of late. Almost certainly the main culprit in the decline of the sea trout has been the proliferation of inshore fish farms. These farms have been responsible for such colossal build-ups of sea lice that sea trout returning to the sea have just not been able to force a way through. In those happy rivers where sea trout are still thriving a great deal of work is being done in understanding these most mysterious of fish. Until recently, the sea trout was considered primarily a fish of the night, and there's no doubt that that is when their principle movements take place. However, increased usage of small wet flies and newly-designed dry flies have shown that sea trout will take freely in the day if pursued with caution and stealth.

◀ **AT REST** This sleek buccaneer of a fish was caught momentarily at rest, just upstream from the sea but still very much in the tidal river. Sea trout usually rest in shelter by day only to travel again at night, but this isn't always the case. On duller days, particularly towards the end of the season, they seem keen to carry on, as though in a hurry to reach the spawning beds.

◀ **A GLORIOUS FISH** A really magnificent sea trout for Johnny Jensen, my great fishing partner and valued collaborator on this book. The sun is setting over the sea behind him, and light is a critical consideration when it comes to sea-trout fishing. However, when we're talking about coastline sea trout, the state of the tide is even more critical. Some pools fish well on an incoming tide, whereas others are at their best on the ebb; it's very much a matter of local experience, but do keep your eyes open for leaping fish – always an obvious giveaway.

Flies in the Kelp

Fly fishing the sea pools is a demanding business. As I've already said, knowledge of the tides is absolutely essential to fishing success and your own personal safety. It's important not to be stranded away from the shoreline as the tide comes in behind you. Also, you'll have to be prepared to make very early starts or stay out late if you're going to get the peak of certain stages of the water. Be prepared, too, to keep on the move when fishing these tidal areas: the fish are swift-moving, feeding here and there, often coming very close into the shore. Cast half a dozen times and then move five or ten yards, but constantly watch for leaping fish. In the darkness, listen for their splashes and home in as quickly as you can. These fish are living on shrimps, small crabs, elvers – quite sizeable food items – so don't be afraid to use large flies worked comparatively quickly.

▶ **FISHING CLOSE TO THE BANK**
Sea trout hunt voraciously in cracks and crannies, prising out items of food, so work your fly in these areas. Let the tide bounce the fly along with its feathers streaming, and get lots of movement in the fly. Sea trout are willing to feed at all levels, so let your fly explore each and every depth zone. A fly around one-and-a-half inches long mimics much of the sea trout's natural prey.

▶ **THROUGH THE WEED**
Alternatively, let your fly sink so it's brushing through the weed beds themselves. It can be infuriating if you keep catching up, but it's worth persevering, for that is where the sea trout expect to find their food. The food items that the sea trout are looking for tend to move in short, sharp bursts, so it's important to work your fly in a similar, twitchy fashion.

The Lochan Brownie

The lochs and lochans in the far north are highly unpredictable. One water, for example, will hold a few large trout, while a water just a few hundred yards away can be infested with weenies. Which water to fish is largely a matter of local knowledge, but you will often come across lochs of which there is no real record whatsoever, and the only thing to do is fish it for yourself. If your first sortie isn't successful, don't give up. These waters can be very temperamental and moody; one fishless afternoon certainly should not mean a loch is written off, far from it – the next trip could be spectacularly successful with fish averaging two pounds or more. As a general rule, kick off with small, skimpy, black flies or, in a good breeze, try skating a large Daddy, for example, across the surface.

◀ **A DISTANT PROMISE** The nature of angling being what it is, the further you're prepared to walk, even in these isolated spots, the better sport you are likely to find. It's a good idea to take a good map with you and even a compass; binoculars can also help. Make sure that you tell somebody where you're setting out to, and don't travel if mist is forecast. These are not places to be taken lightly.

◀ **A JOB DONE** The food supplies on many of these lochs are limited. There will sometimes be rises, especially at terrestrial flies blown onto the water, but many of the browns survive more by digging and foraging than waiting for food to drift past. It pays, therefore, to fish flies deeply and slowly. A small, dark fly just inched along the bottom caught the eye of this small but beautifully-formed brown trout.

FROM THE SEA

Salmon fishing is virtually always a game of waiting and hoping. Everything depends on the fish deciding to leave the sea, cut through the estuaries and begin to climb the rivers. Tides are important but more crucial is the amount of rainfall – salmon just won't ascend skinny water. Fish that are fresh in from the sea are probably the most easily caught of all – they're active and restless and can be seen jumping and splashing. A high tide and a high river are irresistible to them, and it's possible that fish even upstream still somehow relate to the high tide on the seas. Salmon are driven by their instincts and by the changes of their environment: the oxygen content of the water is critical to them, as is any rise or fall in water temperature.

The shots that follow were taken during a four-day period in north Devon. The East Lyn is a small river and that, for me, is its beauty. The pools are intimate enough to see the fish, and individuals proved to be recognizable over an extended period.

▲ **STORM AT SEA** Heavy onshore winds pushed a number of salmon into the Lyn bay, where they attracted the attention of marauding porpoises. Faced with their aggressors, large numbers of grilse decided that the River Lyn was the safer option and they began their ascent of the river much earlier than normal.

Heading Upstream

Salmon on large rivers can move vast distances over the course of twenty-four hours, largely because the river is wide, deep and sufficiently obstacle-free to allow them an easy passage. The Lyn is not like this, rather it consists of endless small pools connected by thin strips of tumbling white water. For these summer grilse, every mile achieved is hard won.

At the start of the excitement, the river was in almost constant flux, with fish moving throughout the daylight hours. In fact, few fish seemed to remain in any single pool for more than two or three hours at a stretch before moving on, ever upwards. Congregations would build up in deep, dark, well-shaded pools, but, inevitably, fish would break out heading through the white water. However, after a couple of days, once the river began to fine down noticeably, daytime activity decreased dramatically. The fish began to sink into lies throughout the daylight hours, and only began to show signs of real restlessness as dusk approached.

◀ **HOLIDAY TOWN** Lynmouth sells its soul to the tourist during the summer season, but that didn't stop the grilse swarming past the car-parks, the pubs, the cafes and the gift shops. Admittedly, their preferred entry times were early and late, but, had the day-trippers known what to look for, fish were present throughout the daylight hours. One of the great beauties of watching fish in the Lyn is the intimacy of the pools. I was able to watch individual fish over the space of two or three days. The salmon had many identifying marks – wounds from nets, lampreys or predators out at sea, a bashed nose or a sliced fin – but above all, the impression of beauty, the fluidity of their movements through the water, their grace and their determined progress upstream remains with me.

▶ **The Waterfall** The East Lyn is studded with waterfalls, not exactly mighty cascades of water but plumes that take some climbing nonetheless. Diving in a waterfall is an intriguing business, the conflicting currents, the shafts of light, the roar of water upon water. Oxygen levels are sky high and these obviously assist the salmon as they strive to pass. The nobility of the species is never more in evidence than at these moments of intense activity – whatever the force of water, salmon will meet the challenge.

▶ **Inside the Fall** We marvel at the way that salmon climb waterfalls, but my own hunch is that there is a kind of escalator system inside the water itself. On the outside, the water quite definitely pours from high to low. However, I do feel there is a sense of reverse flow once you get into the body of the water itself. I believe that salmon – and all migrating fish come to that – have only to find this escalator and they have secured a comparatively easy journey up what is apparently an impassable wall of water.

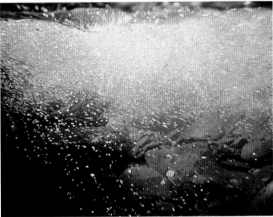

▶ **Another One for the Pot** Some local anglers descended on the East Lyn during the height of the grilse run. They fished as a team tightly and intelligently and caught their quota of salmon, which they took away with them. The bailiff that I talked to saw nothing wrong in this and, after long consideration, I guess he was right. A river should be healthy enough to provide its anglers with a limited number of fish that are going to be eaten and appreciated.

The Salmon in the River

One of the best things about small salmon rivers is that you can watch salmon intimately and study their every twist and turn as they ascend the river. Salmon behave in peculiar ways. One fish struck me in particular: for no apparent reason whatsoever, it spent a good eight hours in a deep pool with its entire body hidden in a crevice between the rocks, only its tail wavering in the current. Other fish formed quite identifiable groups, numbering anything from two to five or six. As a diver, it was also fascinating watching their behaviour when there was any disturbance on the river-bank. Walkers, for example, a hundred yards or so away would instantly begin to agitate a group of fish; a passing group of boys threw some stones in upriver and the knot of salmon I was watching dispersed immediately. These are fish living very much on their nerves, and the more shallow and clear the water, the more twitchy the fish.

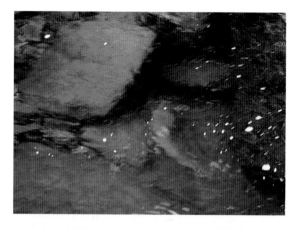

◀ **USING THE ROCKS** Generally, the salmon kept on the move, and it was interesting to watch them make their progress. They often appeared to avoid the main flow, preferring to ease their way on the margins of the current, using every bit of respite the rocks gave them from the full force of the flow. This may seem tortuous but, in actual fact, their progress was extremely rapid using this technique.

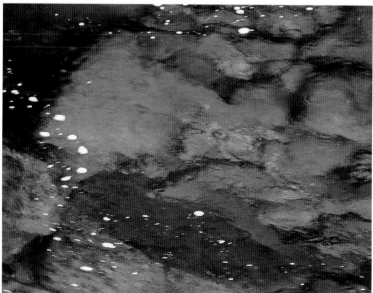

◀ **UNDERSTANDING CURRENTS** Rocks of any size are major factors in the stream. They throw up surprising currents and cross-currents, and often not at all as you'd expect watching from the surface. Also, the calmest piece of water is often upstream of a rock rather than behind it. In fishing terms, the lesson here is glaringly obvious: faced with new water, working your fly around rocks visible either to the eye or by the boils they create on the surface is as good a starting point as you'll find.

The Working of the Fly

Seen in the water, a fly tied of fur and feather looks much more like a living creature than the inanimate, robotic retrieval of a spoon or spinner. Worked properly, a fly can look remarkably like a small, escaping food item. I have grave doubts about whether the most cunningly tied salmon fly ever looks like any food item in particular, but that's not the point: what they do is to look real enough to excite a salmon's interest, aggression or even, perhaps, appetite.

▶ **IN OPEN WATER** A fly worked like this in open water stands out starkly from the natural foodstuffs around it. Few prey items dare risk travelling through featureless areas, especially in daylight, preferring to hug the bottom, weed or submerged rocks. Think carefully about the route any fly will take as you make a retrieve.

▶ **IN COVER** Far better to work your fly around any features in the water. Rocks, as I've previously said, are a must. Look also for any snags, overhanging trees, fallen branches – any structure that breaks a pool up and gives the fly extra movement and life.

▶ **IN THE FLOW** This is where the salmon fly really does begin to explode with life. A fly dangled and worked through white water looks magnificent. You can see why the tail of the pool has always been explored: the push there makes the fly sleek, and skitters it up and down as it travels. These are the keys: think how to make your fly behave naturally but also excitingly; don't fish the water methodically; work your fly with imagination and intelligence.

MONGOLIAN ODYSSEY

The primary target for the angler in Mongolia is the magnificent taiman, a prehistoric member of the salmon family that is now landlocked. Little is known about the taiman, so this is where the travelling angler can play a part in scientific research and help to answer some important questions: how far do taiman travel to spawn? How great is their range? Why do some flaunt red tails and others orange?

A fly rod is a wonderful means of introduction to remote societies. Without the lure of fishing, it's highly doubtful that I would have ever met Batsukh, a northern Mongolian herdsman, and his family. Over the years, a meaningful relationship has built up between the visiting anglers and these people of the plain and the forest. Theirs is a remarkable lifestyle, one of hardship and dignity, and their knowledge of the terrain is extraordinary but then, of course, their very survival depends upon it.

▲ A WORLD OF WONDER In Mongolia, the huge deep pools – many of which hold taiman, as well as rare white fish – burst out into long wild stretches of running water.

The Fish and the Fishing

It is possible to settle on any one of the large pools and make your whole day there but, possibly, if it's taiman you're after it's better to travel light and give yourself the ability to roam. The more water that you can cover during the course of a day, the better chance you have of contacting a pod of these extraordinary fish.

▲ RAPIDS INTO DEEPS These are critical taking places in Mongolia, as predatory fish are sure to be around. The taiman like to hang in deeper water but they make frequent sallies into the shallows to hunt for grayling and trout. Observation over many years indicates that big taiman work together as a pack, channelling trout and grayling into shallows where it's impossible for them to escape.

▶ A HUNTING TAIMAN This is the most exciting of fishing, when you can actually see these large fish, sometimes up to seventy or eighty pounds, cruising the shallow water under bright sunlight. They travel quickly, sometimes in packs, looking for lenok trout and grayling up to four pounds in weight, which they then engulf with awesome ease.

▲ **A Creature of Beauty** Grayling are the main food source of the taiman, but they're also marvellous sport fish. Those found in Mongolia grow to around four pounds in weight and are easily the most stunningly coloured sub-species I have come across. Their dorsal fins are also particularly massive, which allows them to fight hard in the swift currents. Also, unlike other grayling species, they're in the habit of jumping at least a yard from the water on several occasions during the fight.

◄ **The Misunderstood Lenok** Lenok are frequently ignored by visiting anglers, but this is a great error. They are magnificent fish in their own right, and only pale by comparison with the lordly taiman. With their rose-coloured spots along the flank, lenok look somewhat like rainbow trout, but their mouth is much more under-slung, similar to a member of the barbel family. This may enable them to make the most of food stocks that live among the bottom stones; caddis are a favourite food.

Dawn 'til Dusk

The fishing day in Mongolia is a long one. Very frequently, some of the best pools are many miles away from camp and can only be reached by walking or by horse. A start is made soon after breakfast, while the sun is melting the overnight frost. Peak feeding times seem to be around midday and perhaps the first two hours of the afternoon. There is another explosion of activity as the sun sets and darkness creeps in. It can be dangerous to be far from camp once the temperatures plummet and the wolves begin to prowl, but the temptation to keep fishing is enormous: once darkness falls, taiman move from deep water into the shallows where they hunt ravenously for fish and, especially, for marmots, which begin to leave their holes as the sun sets. Many of these little creatures come to drink and even attempt to cross the river where they're picked off by the big fish.

▶ **SMOKING DAWN** As night temperatures plummet, the water cools dramatically and dawn frequently turns the river into a cauldron of mist. The scene has a beauty of its own, but very few fish are caught early. The best fishing is in the early afternoon, once the hot sun has restored a modicum of heat to the shallows. Grayling, in particular, are also very active during this period.

▶ **THE LONELY ANGLER** This photograph really shows what fly fishing a wilderness water is all about. It is a place where you don't see another person, let alone another angler, all day long. A place where there is no footprint on the sand, no litter, no camp-fire… nothing but the vast world encompassing you.

Mongolian Grayling

This extraordinary sub-species of grayling appears to be restricted to an area of north-west Mongolia. They are very beautiful fish, featuring particularly large eyes, a stunning combination of colours down the flanks and, noticeably, a bright golden band to the tail root. The fish average one to two pounds with, abnormally, fish of three to four pounds being caught. Some grayling are virtually coal black, but these are not often seen. In many places, the river absolutely swarms with large grayling and, given the length of the savage winters, it's initially difficult to imagine the rivers holding sufficient food stocks. Undoubtedly, the larger fish are predatorial to some degree, but there's still an extraordinary amount of fly life in the river itself. Stoneflies in particular dominate – these are large insects that often appear in the late afternoon, when there can be a significant rise.

▲ **BOULDERS** Find stones on the bottom of a Mongolian river and you'll find grayling. What you won't be able to do is locate them over the sand and fine gravel reaches. The reason for this is obvious once you turn over the large stones, for that's where you will find the grayling's food – a vast variety of nymph forms, some very large; stoneflies in particular are awesome. When choosing an artificial, anything large, black and heavy worked slowly along the bottom performs well on any piece of water.

▲ **To the River-bank** These grayling can, however, be taken on dry flies even though there is rarely anything like a recognizable hatch. In fact, the time that you're most likely to see grayling dimple the surface is during the late afternoon when breezes frequently blow the larch needles into the margins of the river – grayling that I've killed to eat have been packed with them.

▲ **A Stunning Example** There's little that words can add to this picture. Fish like this make a journey to the end of the earth worthwhile.

Taiman on the Mouse

The Mongolians themselves have a mixed reaction to both fish and fishing. They're great meat eaters and ardent hunters, often travelling for many days at a time through the forest, returning with deer, pig and any other game they can find. If they do fish, which is rarely, it's generally with large nets laid out along the margins of the big, deep pools. They're not after taiman so much – these are big enough to destroy the nets anyway – but they do enjoy a soup made out of white fish, grayling and lenok. One of the few times that they will fish for taiman in any organized fashion is with a hand line, a mouse, a hook and very little else. Ideally, they'll choose a night with a full moon and very little wind. They'll drift the live, squeaking bait down pools of medium depth and a steady current. If a mouse is unavailable, then a squirrel or a marmot will do. Takes are unmissable and the deeply-hooked taiman stands little chance of breaking cord several hundred pounds in breaking strain.

◀ USING A MOUSE Our Mongolian helicopter pilot never misses a chance to fish a river when he's out of Ulan Bataar. Creating the perfect imitation mouse for taiman, which have very good eyesight and sheer away from anything unnatural, is something of an art form. Mind you, strong rumour has it that only a few years ago a big fish was landed on a child's teddy bear! It is important to work any surface lure in the right water. Choose anything too rough and the lure will be drowned.

◀ WORKING THE SHALLOWS The shallows are where the taiman expect the mice to be. It pays to fish them quite quickly in rapid jerks, letting them hang motionless for a few seconds before splashing them on through the surface – the more commotion, the better. Large surface poppers also do the trick. Choose propeller baits or chuggers that really plough up the surface.

▶ **Closing In** A marauding taiman has a terrifying burst of pace and covers five yards in the twinkling of an eye. They also show great discrimination and frequently veer off even when a take seems absolutely certain. When fish compete, then your chance is higher, as it is in any form of fly fishing. Show your mouse to a pod of four or five fish and a take is virtually guaranteed.

▶ **A Piscatorial Torpedo** Taiman show no fear of travelling in water so shallow that their backs ride clear. The thrill of the chase obviously grabs them and, although a member of the salmon family, they are as aggressively predatorial as any pike. A normal taiman lie will be around a big rock out in mid-river, often in very deep water. This is where they rest: they're aware of any dead fish coming down with the drift and will move out to take them, but it's in the shallows that they show their most aggressive feeding behaviour.

▶ **The Eye of the Hunter** The large eye of the taiman is ideally suited for picking out prey, even when the water clouds during the summer rains. Also, as many taiman hunt hard at night, it is vital for them to be able to utilize any light the moon sheds. Wild fish such as this are quickly aware of movement on the bank, so take great care with your approach and, especially, your casting.

Taiman on the Fly

Although many big taiman are caught on bait and spinners, fly fishing is undoubtedly the most exciting method... and it works. You will need to wade so that you can cover the best water and it's essential to use streamer flies of at least four or five inches in length. Ten-weight gear is generally sufficient, although leaders should be at least thirty pounds breaking strain. It's also a good idea to use a light wire trace of some nine or twelve inches in length. Taiman have very sharp teeth indeed and can, if you are unlucky, sever mono-filament.

Ideal fly water will probably be a long run, anything between two and six feet deep. Work the water comparatively quickly: if a taiman is going to take, it will probably do so the very moment it sees a lure go past. Floating lines are probably sufficient, but there's often keen wind on the rivers, so a weight-forward line helps casting in these conditions. Whatever you do, make sure that your reel has plenty of backing; if a big fish gets out in the current, it can easily run off a couple of hundred yards of line.

▲ Hooked Streamer flies are best worked among the rocks, frequently near overhangs and ledges, the sorts of places where taiman lurk. The times I've been able to get beneath the surface, I've rarely seen them out in the full flow, rather they make the best use they can of any cover. Don't worry if your fly frequently catches on the boulders – this is where the taiman will be lurking.

▶ **A WORTHY FISH** Reuben certainly deserved this glorious taiman that he took in the early afternoon just before a flurry of snow drifted up the valley. Cold weather frequently stimulates the taiman into a feeding frenzy – it's as though they sense that winter is on the way.

▼ **UP TOP** Very big fish like this frequently feed near the surface, where they are looking for mice and marmots crossing the river. They will also take fallen birds, squirrels, and even fallen bats at dusk. This taiman was taken on a sparsely-tied streamer fly fished near the surface to produce an attractive wake.

TOTAL FLY FISHING

As I said earlier, I truly believe there's barely a fish that swims that can't be caught on a fly – there are only conditions that militate against fly fishing. Certainly every species that I've watched beneath the surface has fed on food items that can be quite easily replicated. I'm a great believer in the fly as a weapon: tied skilfully, a creation of fur and feather works so much better down in the water than a relatively inanimate piece of metal, wood or plastic. All predators – for example, perch, pike, bass – eat fish, and we know that flies can be tied to look like fish. The non-predatory species – generally members of the cypronid family, such as carp, tench and barbel – eat all manner of small aquatic insects such as caddis, shrimp and beetles, and, once again, we have exactly the patterns for those. Much the same holds true for a range of sea fish, too.

It's a shame that more bait fishermen don't realize the possibilities – fly fishing is simply so much more mobile and exciting than sitting static over bait. Equally, it's a shame more trout fishermen don't realize the fun that other so-called 'lesser' species can give on the fly. Until you've hooked a big carp on a fly rod, you don't know what a fight is!

◀ **POT OF GOLD** Niels, a brilliant Danish fly angler, took this perfect rudd from the waters of the Ural delta on a tiny imitation. The crystal-clear lagoons were perfect for the fly.

Bream

If ever there was a day that changed my fishing life it was one in June 1998 spent in the company of Franta, a Czech fly-fishing international. We were on his home river in Bohemia, a river full of trout, grayling, bream, barbel and a few very nice-sized common carp. The water averaged between three and five feet in depth with some deeper pools. I was bait fishing for the barbel, while Franta was wandering the river with his traditional nymph fishing outfit. He was primarily after the trout and the grayling but, he assured me, virtually anything could come along.

▶ **THE MYSTERY BREAM** It didn't work out like that though. I'd been bait fishing a weir for a couple of hours, experiencing all manner of frustrating line bites. I pulled out, Franta moved in, and within two casts had netted a four-pound bream taken on a caddis imitation bounced along the bottom. I was stunned – Franta was not. His team of three deep-fished nymphs raked the bottom, picking up any feeding fish (see page 57). Total control is, however, essential.

▶ **THE DAY OF MIRACLES** So it went on. Franta wandered down the river, unencumbered with the tackle I needed as a bait fisherman. He stopped here and there, working his flies down any of the deeper glides. He picked up trout, grayling, more bream, barbel and even a small common carp. At the end of the day, I'd been totally out-fished by the Czech nymph-fishing technique practised by a master of the method.

Pike

Pike on the fly is not news these days but, over the last five or ten years, has become an acknowledged method. Given the right conditions, fly fishing for pike can be just as effective as using lures – even more so given the flies' fluidity in the water. It's important to choose your first pike fly waters carefully: don't go for waters that are too deep with a small head of fish. Instead, concentrate on shallower, more prolific venues. Weather, too, is vital. Begin your fly fishing in the warmer months, spring and autumn especially, when the fish are on the shallows hunting among reed beds. Summertime is also good, particularly around lilies and other patches of floating weed. Give yourself a chance to catch some average pike on the fly before setting yourself bigger challenges. Confidence is important and it's essential that you build up reserves of experience for the harder tasks to come. Aim for what US anglers call the 'pattern' – the right fly fished in the right place at the right depth at the right speed.

▲ **BALTIC PIKE** There are things you have to remember, however. First and foremost, the water must be comparatively clear. From observations under the surface, I believe that you need visibility of at least three yards before fishing the fly becomes a truly practical project. Warmer water also helps, as the fish are likely to be particularly wired-up and aggressive.

▶ **SOME CONSIDERATIONS** Polaroid glasses are almost an essential, both for spotting pike and for watching the progress of your fly. If the fly doesn't look to be working correctly, change it. Chestwaders are also a good idea. In shallow, reedy waters like this, you can get yourself into a prime position. Don't think you need to go too over-gunned for pike: I've made do with an eight-weight outfit quite easily.

▶ **THE WIRE TRACE** Whatever you do, always ensure that you put a wire trace on any fly designed to look like a small fish, even if you're bass or perch fishing and there are pike and/or zander in the water. The sharp teeth of these latter two species will almost instantly slice through nylon, and leaving a fly in a fish is to be avoided at all costs.

▶ **JUST A GLIMPSE** A pike might be impulsive when it's hungry but it's still not stupid. Work your fly with every bit as much thought as you would when you're trout fishing. Work it in spurts; let it rest; let it sink and lie on the bottom; move it off in small, sand-puffing jerks; even let it rest on the top side of a lily pad, for example, with just a few of its feathers visible from below.

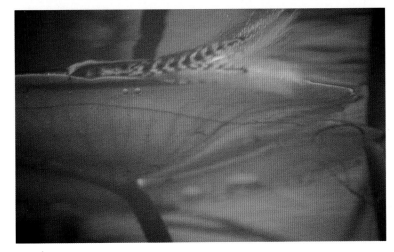

◀ **THE MOUSE** It's situations like this that offer new, exciting possibilities. Why not try something out of the ordinary and bomb the fish with a big mouse pattern – this one is around six inches long from nose to tail. Work it thoughtfully: pull it back in six-to twelve-inch jerks, then just let it hang, sending out small ripples across the surface. You'll almost certainly see signs of interest from the fish, and when one makes up its mind the take can be explosive.

▼ **IN THE SHALLOWS** If your lake or river has marginal shallows, patrolling them very carefully can pay dividends, either by walking along the river-bank or getting out in a boat. If you can see a pike, especially during the warmer months, the chances are you can catch it. Watch the pike's body language: if its pectorals are moving, it's alert; if its eye moves, then it's watching.

Barbel

Let's put it simply: if you can catch barbel on the fly, then you can catch anything this way. Barbel feed deep, combing the bottom in a very slow, methodical fashion and this makes them a difficult target. The photographs that follow were taken out in Spain, which makes the job that much easier – the warmer the water, the more likely barbel of any sub-species are to feed enthusiastically. Also, Spanish barbel suffer from very little angling pressure and this makes them that much more naïve. However, barbel can also be taken on the fly in the colder, more pressured waters of the United Kingdom and other parts of northern Europe. It can be difficult but, given the right water and the right conditions, you will have success. Summer and early autumn are the best times and you need water with good visibility. Choose a run that is no deeper than six feet; with any luck, you'll be close to your fish and you'll actually be able to see them. Work a team of two or three nymphs down among the feeding fish, concentrate very hard and strike at any indication that the barbel has moved to intercept a fly.

▲ CAMOUFLAGE? Should I be wearing that shirt, reflecting the light so brightly? Years of experience both on the bank and on the river-bed still haven't answered that particular question for me. My hunch is that fish see shapes and shadows rather than colours above the surface.

◀ **THE STRIKE** Watch your fly very closely indeed because barbel have the ability to suck it in and blow it out again before you know it. A fly some two or three inches from a barbel snout can disappear in the blink of an eye. Strike indicators can sometimes work, but very frequently the fly is out before the indicator has even dipped. It's far better if you can watch exactly what's going on.

◀ **THE TAKE** It's very rare indeed to get a fly-caught barbel that's hooked in anything but the extremities of the lip. It's also very important to watch their reaction to different flies. Most, they'll ignore altogether. Some, they'll swing across the current to investigate. Just a few – and the menu changes from day to day – excite a proper response.

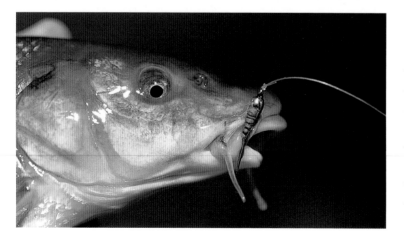

◀ **THE FLY** If I had to settle for anything, it would probably be a goldhead of some description. There's no doubt about it – the gleam that the bead gives off seems to be an attractor. However, there are times when that shine has the opposite effect and actually scares the fish. If you sense this, change to a large, dark nymph.

Bass

It's quite easy to see why Americans adore their bass fishing so much. Bass are beautiful, fight well and offer one of the most extraordinary challenges any fly fisherman is likely to meet. The point about bass is that they are exceptionally inquisitive and will come to investigate fly pattern after fly pattern – nearly always without making a decision either to accept or reject. It obviously helps to fish clear water where you can see the reaction of the bass to any particular fly pattern. If you're fishing by feel, then sensitive fingers are a necessity; a bass can suck in a fly and hang with it for seconds without moving and then, puff... the fly is out, the bass is gone and the angler knows next to nothing about it.

▶ **THE BASS MOUTH** You'd think that when a bass, large-mouth or small, opens those cavernous jaws it's going to mean business. You're right, but only once it's made its mind up. My experience of watching bass under water only backs up what every experienced angler knows: bass are inquisitive, great investigators, clear-sighted, cautious, cunning and very discriminating. Keep experimenting with your flies and the way you work them.

▶ **THE MARGINS** Most of my serious bass fishing has taken place in the lakes of Spain, and I've never felt more confident than working the margins of these great waters, especially in the mornings before the light sends the bass deeper. If you've got a boat, great, but use it to seek out mid-lake islands or rocky outcrops – the key to bass fishing is finding the cover.

◀ **WHERE BASS LIVE** Bass, as I've discovered, will choose anywhere – even the skull of a long-dead farm animal! Everything from dumped shopping trolleys to crashed, sunken cars will prove to be a magnet. If you don't dive, then spend as much time as possible exploring the waters for the structures that bass adore.

◀ **ROCK HOPPING** You won't often find bass far from rocks; they just love them. Rocks offer shade, security, ambush potential and a veritable feasting ground. Other top places include natural features, such as stream inlets, fallen trees and weed beds. Human influence can help – work dam walls, water towers and jetties with care.

◀ **DIGGING** What you will notice about bass if you spend time watching them is their ferocity. They'll not only chase insects and fish through the water but they're also happy to get digging for a good square meal. In the Spanish waters that I fish, crayfish are especially welcome and bass will often move quite large stones to get at a fleeing crustacean.

▶ **THE ATTACK** A fly is taken with great gusto and the bottom silt is lifted by the force of the fish bellying. It's also interesting just to look at that battered nose and imagine what may have caused it – a fight? A tangle with a crayfish? Wear and tear from its digging activities? Almost certainly the damage was done by the bass diving into the rocks and rubbing its head there in an attempt to dislodge the fly. Sometimes you'll catch a fish with similar wounds healed but reopened in another battle.

▲ **MASTER BASS** The bass is an intelligent, challenging opponent, both wary and aggressive in equal degrees. The modern US bass masters are constantly aware of the need to change the approach on a hard day; relax and you are lost. And a last tip: to stop a bass jumping and throwing the hook, try burying the tip of the rod beneath the surface of the water.

Bonefish in the Bahamas

Pound for pound, you won't find any fish catchable on the fly fighting harder than the bonefish. When I first read the American books on the art, I dismissed the stories surrounding that first, phenomenal, notorious run. How on earth could any four-pound fish break ten-pound leaders with such contemptuous ease? Well, they can. Try to slow them down if you wish, but to stop them... forget it. Their torpedo-like shape, musculature and large fins allow them to reach speeds well in excess of twenty miles per hour. The most exciting aspect of bonefishing, though, is trying to understand these creatures, their relationship with the tides, the wind patterns and the depth and bottom make-up of their feeding grounds. To watch a shoal of a couple of hundred bonefish working their way towards you along a flat is one of the most exciting experiences possible. You know that any false move on your part is going to send the fish fleeing in panic in such skinny water.

◀ **THE FLATS** These shallow, warm, food-rich areas of the Caribbean are the natural home of the bonefish. They follow the tides and the winds, covering vast regions of ground as they seek shrimps, crabs and small fish. This is a huge, ever-changing world, and mobility on the part of the angler is vital.

◀ **THE HUNT** You can fish for bonefish from boats and this often proves effective. However, I prefer to walk, ideally behind an experienced guide who knows exactly when, where and why a particular area will attract a head of fish. Walk very carefully, wear Polaroids and scan the water in front of you intently for these fish that move like ghosts.

▶ **Grubbing** If you're very lucky, you will stumble across fish in crystal-clear water stirring up the bottom, feeding hard. Don't put a fly too close to a bonefish – the line will almost immediately spook it. Cast beyond it and work the fly back slowly until the fish sees it, generally between six and twelve inches away. Don't be in too much of a hurry to work a fly fast – let it settle on the bottom for seconds at a time before twitching it onward.

▶ **Perfection** Built like Concorde, the big-nosed, sleek-shaped bonefish is elegantly constructed for speed. The silvery scales, too, serve their purpose – seen below, in gin-clear water under a shimmering sun, a school of bones glints mesmerizingly in front of your eyes. It's impossible to pick out individual fish, and I guess any passing shark finds it hard to guarantee a successful strike.

▶ **The Guides** Scotland, Europe, New Zealand, Montana… it doesn't matter where in the world you're fly fishing, take the advice of the men on the spot as these are the people who know the fish, the waters and the styles. Fidel has learnt everything he knows about bonefish – and that's pretty well all there is to know – from father Amos, and no doubt Fidel will pass that knowledge on to at least one of his seven sons!

The European Coast

Increasingly, fly anglers are beginning to realize the opportunities offered by the seashore. In relatively calm, clear seas a fly can score heavily, especially with mobile, sporting species. Mullet, bass, wrasse and mackerel all make a perfect change for the angler jaded with the ubiquitous rainbow trout.

◀ **THE MULLET** Mullet swarm around virtually every European coastline throughout the summer and often move up the tidal stretches of rivers. They can be infuriating to catch on bait, but they suddenly become easy in shallow, relatively clear water on small, goldhead nymphs. Try and get to them just as the tide is coming in, filling shallow lagoons where they like to grub for food.

▲ **SEA BASS** Perhaps best of all that the sea can offer is a bass on the fly at sunset as the day is beginning to cool. Bass will come as close as a rod length from the shore, hunting among the surf for countless food items. Try a small, silver lure, perhaps one or two inches long, worked quite quickly in water that's often no more than a yard deep. Takes can be explosive, and where there's one fish you can expect more.

▶ **BABY BASS** Recent results suggest that the bass stocks around the European coasts are steadily on the rise. This shot of young bass was taken off the Spanish coast – very large fish make their way up the tributaries of rivers there and throughout most of Europe. Watch for the commotion as they hunt small fish, and put a silver streamer fly to them.

▲ **MACKEREL MARGIN** Mackerel can provide the most exciting sport on the fly rod. They are especially active in the warmer months, coming within feet of rocky headlands. Fish small streamers and keep mobile until you find patrol routes. Never use more than one fly, as if you use a team, a fly rod can easily be smashed.

Author's Acknowledgements

My greatest thanks for encouragement, inspiration, generosity and friendship go to Johnny Jensen and Martin Hayward Smith; both are expert photographers who have collaborated with me so closely on these works – I cannot possibly overstate their contribution.

Thank you also to Kevin Cullimore for showing me the way, back in the 1990s. Thank you to the late and dearly missed Mike Smith at Bure Valley Fisheries, Mike Taylor at the Red Lion in Bredwardine, Bill Makins at Pensthorpe and Paul Seaman for all your help with locations.

Thank you in Spain to Peter, Rafa, Ignatio and José… marvellous men and anglers all.

Thank you to all the following for your help either in fishing situations or for your copious and wise advice: Alan Felstead, Leo Grosze Nipper, Sue and Chris Harris, Reuben Hook, Phil Humm, Simon MacMillan, Robert Malone, Rob Olsen, Christopher West and Jo Whorisky.

Thank you to Steve at Ocean Optronics, and to Fergus Granville in North Uist.

Thank you to all at Design Revolution, and special thanks to Carol, who has had to contend with a mass of woolly-minded thoughts from yours truly.